RAMPTON
MAD
WORLD

SCOTIA WAKELYNN

Typeset in Chaparral Pro

Editing, design, typesetting and publishing by UK Book Publishing

www.ukbookpublishing.com

ISBN: 978-1-913179-58-8

RAMPTON
MAD
WORLD

RAMPTON
MAD WORLD

The reason for writing this book was due to many factors that I witnessed in fifteen years employed at Rampton Hospital. However, it's the last four years where something fundamental has completely disappeared from Rampton altogether. The more experiences I had the more questions it would raise and in many ways the place is very unique and probably can't be compared to anywhere else in the country.

I am not the first to write a book about Rampton – one was written by a patient as far back in the nineteen fifties. And as far as I am aware this is not the first one written by a staff member either. However, the other books were written in different decades and as the pendulum of supposed Hard time (under the Home Office) swung to what's now considered liberalised Hotel time. This book comes from an era where the Asylum is now in the hands of the mad, and I'm not necessarily on about the patients either.

There are things that take place here and have to be dealt with that happen nowhere else in the country and although at times inexcusable, situations and incidents can be unique without a precedent of another institute. However, I have a confession to make if there is one. I wrote this book whilst on suspension from Rampton. In my view for basically whistle blowing and when that had been covered up for putting a protest in writing and internally circulating it. Although I felt better afterwards, and the sustained absence helped put things into perspective outside the goldfish bowl of the Asylum, inevitably being outspoken made me vulnerable to a backlash and a formal form of ostracism was imposed. This is the time when I realised speaking the truth will not protect you and principles will always cost you. But what I also noticed was the truth does echo. Many staff had to cross the street to make a remark about my comments and the overriding factor was it was all true.

The suspension letter hinged on the fact that being removed from work would prevent me from circulating information further around the Hospital. The irony here is it did not concern itself with whether the document was fact, and one of the few positives of my suspension was that it actually raised my written comments profile and quite possibly staff were more enticed to read my Newsletter than if I hadn't been suspended at all. Better still, if a manager had just pulled me into an office and asked outright about the content and whether it came from me, I would have openly confessed. After all, I have done nothing wrong and have nothing to hide and I stand by everything I have written. Since then it would have only appeared in a document, but now parts of it have been exposed by the press where others have come forward and now it forms part of a very public post-mortem in the form of a comprehensive book.

The long days of suspension meandered into weeks then months as I subconsciously descended into a depression of uncertainty. Being alienated from work, which until then had taken up my entire life for so long. Usually fifty to sixty hours a week. It was initially hard to make the adjustment and my job remained on perpetual death row with a gagging order as part of the conditions. That meant I was unable to talk about it until someone from work could be bothered to contact me. That eventually came with correspondence from the investigator 76 days into the suspension and between us we organised a date to meet. But that did not stop him going away on holiday for weeks before we could pin down a specific day. It's incredulous that someone was allowed to keep my suspension pending. Why would somebody employ a person with annual leave coming up and why would he accept it? It just goes to show suspensions are much more than people first realise.

The words that staff use to describe having endured a suspension or witnessed staff colleagues on suspension at Rampton can range from, a holding action, a restraining order, institutionalised bullying, a punitive measure and the power of domestic internment. The outcome of which renders you, for a sustained duration, a phantom employee. I would like to add to this list that Rampton suspend staff as a form of passive resistance. Something we would usually associate with patients who refuse to cooperate with staff socially or become a deadweight when carried to seclusion.

They win when they make you think you're alone.

In my view suspensions are a new phenomenon and are now a common reaction for senior managers when they want to eliminate any opposition of staff. And in my experience it is definitely used as a punitive measure. It is deliberately protracted as well so that they have full unregulated control. It's a calculated advertisement to let all Rampton employees know who's in charge and that this is what happens to staff displaying what they consider to be insubordination. It is also a power struggle to let me, the individual, know they can do what they want when they want and they are right because they have.

The length of time taken to suspend staff suggests that there may have been occasions where there were interludes or working on my suspension case, but I sincerely believe there were many more weeks where no effort was made in bringing the case to a close. At the very least managers do not alter their working diaries, still take booked vacation weeks at a time. Their working lives are not inconvenienced or postponed because of an added suspension. This is why I know that my suspension was never reviewed although policy states it is meant to be every fourteen days. You don't get any letters that break down the reasons for remaining suspended. Once you are off you are made to stay off.

Eight months' suspension for circulating information just doesn't warrant it. And that was confirmed the day the investigation report hit my doormat. Not an indentation as the dossier crashed on the floor with a thud. No reams of documents, more of a pamphlet. The six statements, none of them extensive, had all been completed by June 2019, which was more than four months before somebody bothered to post it. I think it is a good argument also that once a suspension reaches a landmark time then to me its validity and authenticity fades into insignificance and that would account for mine and the majority of Rampton suspensions. Equally to weigh the suspension against the alleged offence should impact on the final punishment but it doesn't. Being suspended for six months or a year makes absolutely no difference to an outcome.

"Rumour is the murmur of something said whether truth or lie"

I can safely say staff suspensions are never confidential – there are too many people on all upper levels who leak information and I think to a degree they are meant to. This became very apparent in several managers' statements during my investigation, that they had obtained confidential information about me to aid their statements and prior to interview – an employee's Personal Information should be stored in a way that they should have no access to. Equally the two independent investigators who spoke to me were open and honest and admitted that a preconceived approach and attitude towards me had already been conveyed to them by my senior managers so it was hard for them to remain impartial when they had been told things about me already to alter their opinion. The impression I got for the friendly disclosure from them was that what they had been told did not match the person sat in front of them.

The other thing is the person who suspended me doesn't know me and sits six tiers above my position and this information is automatically cascaded down my immediate line management structure. Then the information – or in this case misinformation – goes viral as it literally seeps out and becomes known throughout all levels at work which is what happened to my case. By the time the first week had passed I walked down to my local town centre, East Retford, and the general rumour was already hospital-wide that I had been sacked. I believe in hindsight there was a devious and calculated reason for this. It was important for Rampton to publicly convey a particular message. After all, they do not want mainstream staff speaking out or telling more home truths and in doing so informing people that I had been sacked kept the masses in check. There are over two thousand employed at what is the biggest high secure Psychiatric hospital this side of the Urals.

Time will give no indication of the outcome either. I know of staff who were suspended for a full year and then unceremoniously sacked. Why on earth would you take a year to sack somebody? Surely the suspension has to be taken into consideration? Or the financial hardship of being on reduced pay for a whole year? But it isn't. Your working world or career is on complete hold until such time somebody has had enough of sticking a pin in you like a voodoo doll and eventually thrust a sword in instead. This is one of the many forms of punishment to hand to what we are told, by Rampton, is meant to be a priority procedure.

Again the conscientious employer should, under normal rational circumstances, need to get to the bottom of a situation for the sake of the name of the organisation or at least restoring trust . It also has to be seen to be taking an incident seriously and the general amount of time taken suggests otherwise. And this is where the 28-day suspension policy lays dormant in a folder on a shelf somewhere. A document that was once negotiated and agreed amongst personnel and union representatives years ago has now been consigned to archives. A document flouted to the point it is practically out of existence. That the negotiation of such a document indicates its inception came from a time when there used to be a professional working relationship between groups of people like staff and unions and unions with managers – but that's all gone now. This comes with a numerical disadvantage in that there aren't many union reps at Rampton anymore, but there are many more managers. Because the 28-day suspension is not live once it reaches day 29, I would argue that any managerial counsel thereafter is beyond conventional jurisdiction and thus has no real legitimate authority to continue.

Contrary to a standard suspension letter from my employer there was no counselling service although I booked on it almost immediately once suspended. There was apparently a considerable waiting list which ran into months and I thought, actually I'm not surprised. All the evidence is already there under a thin veneer of pretences.

The validity of the suspension was to me questionable – after all, it was not something I did as part of my job description and the allegation did not affect my work directly. However, my understanding and empathy for a suspension waned quickly enough when contact remained just three standard letters in the first three months. And besides, there just wasn't enough in my case to legislate for being off work for eight whole months. Somebody was not working on my investigation every single day. Staff were interviewed, as was I – twice, in fact – but that still left many months waiting to be called in.

Considering what I already knew about lengthy staff suspensions I had joined a list of others at Rampton who had been unfortunately removed from their place of work for reasons that to me were unwarranted, disproportionate and often inaccurate. This is where staff are guilty until proven innocent. Where the lack of common sense had disregarded relevant mitigating circumstances that could have been addressed appropriately at work. Some staff were suspended for saying something regarding alleged inappropriate handling techniques in a patient restraint. When a patient is struggling it can be a difficult procedure to get right, especially when there are insufficient staff numbers to get hold of patients' limbs. This is where if a patient has been wronged they are considered victims, but if staff are injured or hurt they are automatically considered incompetent staff.

Another case was over a patient's complaint, others over working practices. Things that possibly could be dealt with more sensitively and immediately, or where the employee could at the very least be relocated to another department or ward but at least kept at work for a time whilst an investigation takes place. I have known staff who have been suspended on the strength of an allegation of a convicted offender as well as being a mentally ill patient. This is how crass Rampton has become. Some staff who I know personally have been suspended at Rampton and given a provisional notification of an allegation as a reason. Had been off for many months then one day out of the blue they were just called back by a phone call from a manager without any reason, apology, nothing. There is also a percentage of suspensions take place unofficially all the time where an allegation has been made and managers automatically suspend, then a week later they have found an alternative placement within Rampton Asylum. Usually where there isn't any patient contact but the staff member's working conditions have been turned upside down because the shifts that they had already agreed to work on the wards are not honoured anymore. Somehow they are expected to abandon that agreed work pattern and work completely different shifts instead. The member of staff is reinstated to this new set of conditions minus a recognition letter explaining the reason for the initial suspension, thus no record of it exists. The staff member who has been placed in a department that works nine to five is unable to honour their rota for a period of time. It's another statistic that becomes a malleable piece of misinformation. The investigation continues but the starting point has been moved to when the staff member was returned to work, and that's under a new set of working conditions, not when they were suspended the week before.

Anyway, irrespective of allegations made, Rampton suspensions have absolutely no urgency for justice or any motivation to prove someone innocent. It is at a manager's leisure to place you on a recreational journey. To me it's usually unjustified where somebody is removed from work under the guise of the Conduct policy. This Trust-wide policy is not a comprehensive document. It does give written instructions or list a logical and rational consideration for things like, do the actions of an individual affect their duties, security or running of the wards. The conduct policy does not highlight infringements or supposed breaches, quoted in a section. The Conduct policy itself is completely empty of samples or examples and does not even have a list of potential misconducts, what constitutes serious or minor conduct. It's a lot more vague than that. It is purely based on the discretion of a manager in what they consider a conduct matter. These whims have no basis in equity, which is why it's usually activated unfairly.

Nobody appears interested in processing somebody with pace so the individual can return to their place of employment whether guilty or not guilty. After all, the impact of such a decision is where somebody else has to be temporarily employed as a replacement usually on overtime rate to cover the shortfall, and it all just goes on and on for months. Equally if somebody is guilty and needs dealing with, somebody should bring it to a quick conclusion for the sake of the public purse. But this is part of the process in attritionally beating you into submission. Instead, although paid, you are made to feel forgotten almost to the point you left but nobody could be bothered to tell you. Then out of the blue an unfamiliar telephone number appears on your caller display and it's a cheerful investigator ringing to meet with you.

It makes you wonder the total annual expenditure of suspending people at Rampton for what is a common – when I say common I mean a daily – and protracted exercise. I presume there isn't a standard budget for something that cannot be predicted. Firstly they remove an employee and find a temporary replacement. When I say 'temporary' I am being facetious. There are staff who have been suspended for as long as eighteen months. Then someone has to locate and employ an investigator who is usually on a zero-hour contract. Many have other investigations or, as I found out, are not available because of annual leave. He or she will then need to interview relevant people all within their work's time so these people will postpone their duties to facilitate an investigation. That's more additional replacements, or more usually their duties are placed on hold.

An investigator needs time to compile evidence and a case, which will need a report, get you to sign it and agree to the statement. Once done this is sent to the commissioning officer – that's the person who decided to suspend and investigate you. Meanwhile the employee who's been suspended will probably, like me, be left in deliberate limbo, without support; become anxious; suffer sleep deprivation, often to the point of insomnia; be interviewed for the considered heinous crime under a Terms of reference – in this case for having an alternative opinion; attend an occupational health appointment; and book on a counselling service, usually six sessions. You have become a manufactured mental health case just like the patients. And Rampton is the apex in the field of mental health, so as far as I'm concerned, if anyone deteriorates because of the way this institute conducts itself, this has to be considered sinister and deliberate.

I doubt there is a manager directly affected anywhere on any ward or in other departments here brave enough to question the blank chequebook budget for generating one of many suspensions, which I suspect is just one insane decision by one ludicrous person. The natural but deliberate expansion of work drawing in from many various departments to fund just one single suspended person deliberately for many months. This to me is one of the most abused and absurd parts of managerial discretion. This is a public organisation, and whether we like it we condone it, and by condoning it I mean we are paying for it.

In my view, if an organisation is run well then suspensions would be an embarrassing thing and lessons would be learned, but there is no shame in the shame at Rampton. It's completely acceptable to inflate a situation, remove staff, disrupt more than one service, mobilise an extra-curricular process for the benefit of who knows.

Years ago when I was still relatively new the approach of suspending everyone and everything for any reason was virtually non-existent. Now it's part of an average person's working life. They will either experience it often many times or know somebody who has. It's not confidential either – nothing ever is in Rampton – but it's seldom made official, either. However, as I have already mentioned the person who suspended me was six tiers above. Nevertheless, rumour fever takes over and I've been inundated with well-wishers wondering how I was coping. It's not nice having an answer for everyone but unless you become a recluse or live away in the country, you have to deal with it and with that means you've got to think about it when you might not want to.

My conclusion in all this is that Rampton's main problem is it resides in the public sector and the private sector generally act better for one basic reason and that's accountability for money. If a private organisation is fined or has to pay out compensation to individuals, this affects budgets and profit directly. It could also affect a contract or service agreement between two companies. At Rampton, however, it's the public purse that foots the bill on every single level including any extra pay outs and that stinks on many levels. Nobody gets to find out the outcome of fines or compensation claims or any pay outs as they are confidential, and this helps the unprofessional and incompetent to keep it away from scrutiny and public view. Rampton and the NHS as a whole makes nationalisation of services look like a broken model, when really it is the aspect of accountability that appears lacking. I am a massive fan of the National Health Service but my experiences have unearthed the reasons why it is in financial turmoil.

And reflecting on my latest events I came to the conclusion that putting my experiences down on paper was maybe a form of closure – or at least a coping strategy for the absurdities that continue relentlessly at Rampton. And at the time, once the book got under way and I could begin to log and analyse the issues and aspects, then categorise the things as I wrote, I began to realise the gravity of what became a conveyer belt of crass anomalies which formed an ever expanding shitty snowball.

The book was also becoming one of the world's longest letters of resignation. The ink being spilt took me to a point of no return. Irrespective of the trajectory of how my job at Rampton was going to end, I had decided that it had to end regardless. It was frustration and despair that drove me to start challenging things in the first place. I initially started it in the formal process but when that was ignored it led me to write about it informally as well. So many incredulous accounts and situations. The important thing here is the elaborate situations suggest you could not make it up. Although I work in a place with plenty of mental material, my imagination isn't that wild. It took time for Rampton to get in the state that it is now in and it will take time to get out of it, if it wants to, that is, and under the current regime it's going nowhere. At the time of writing, 2020, Rampton is now in its fourth abysmal Care Quality Commission report, which has highlighted the same problems over and over again to the point of a perennial nettle.

For one thing, Rampton is a publicly funded organisation under the umbrella of the National Health Service, yes the NHS, but here at Rampton it is run very privately. And this constantly vexes me. I also found during my time here, members of the public generally have a misconception of how Rampton is run and the type of people it cares for. And with that Mr and Mrs Joe Taxpayer do not really know or understand the amount of money that is squandered at Rampton, what it is spent on, who and why. Society has an ignorant trust that once you have read this book, it bears little logical and rational justification. And I suspect a lot of people will say they just didn't realise. I also expect many colleagues to have better horror stories than the ones I have written about. Every working day has a story that by its prevalence and frequency becomes not only believable but institutionally acceptable. Due to its frequency the workforce may be desensitised, but I believe their conscience is still flagging up wrongs in the form of verbal graffiti. That's general gossip, usually circulated by people who are unofficially protesting about the way an incident or situation was dealt with. It normally peters out within a couple of weeks, usually because something else has grabbed the workforce's attention.

Experience is the cheaper form of qualification about a subject with the expense of time

This book is a personal, reflective, practical account based on 15 years of one man's experience in an institute that holds a special exclusive national identity for housing particularly dangerous people. People like Bruce G P Lee, Charles Bronson, Beverley Allett and Ian Huntly have all come through here. Rampton can brag about being an apex institute for seriously dangerous men and women who often have multiple mental disorders. Within those years I worked on every single shift on every single ward, but in the main I was based full time on only four of them and in another department.

Rampton is not a place of mystery although it enjoys trying to be mysterious. It doesn't contain remorseful souls, it isn't like Area 51 where what goes on is top secret. It is not the cutting edge of social science, although having access to the most high profile patients with the most alarming behaviours. The exclusivity of this institute's professional fraternity have a lot more freedom in comparison to other places. But working at Rampton is a great thing to have on your Curriculum Vitae. For a start it was the reason I found another job because my new employers and employees were intrigued by how convicted psychopaths are managed. Rampton is not shrouded in secrecy although I know of those who attempt to prevent any negative Rampton exposure at all, and out of some kind of misguided loyalty they perpetually attempt to preserve this. There was a time when working at Rampton you had to sign the Official Secrets Act and just maybe this nostalgic loyalty, subconsciously curtails a lot of staff especially the older ones from publicising incidents more often. If you do not know what you can and can't say then people stay cautious and tend to just say nothing. A very comprehensive culture of fear binds most mouths shut and presides over any honest conscience when it comes to speaking your mind. Staff do complain like me whilst walking the corridors and in ward handovers all the time, but rarely will anyone do it officially.

That's a landscape filled with ravines of retribution from above that could have you relocated to another less desirable ward, the land mines of being continuously moved around the hospital on any shift so you cannot settle. Being targeted to the point it's obvious and brazen. And, you guessed it, being perpetually suspended. Despite a policy sat on a shelf saying that people are treated fairly and respectfully that has absolutely nothing to do with how staff are managed or how Rampton really runs the hospital and conducts itself internally. There are staff at Rampton who have spent decades in the same place, tucked away on a sedentary ward which is run more like a gentlemen's club. Whilst others may get moved daily and on top of that relocated altogether annually to a succession of volatile and demanding wards and the irony is your pay is the same wherever you are placed. It's another thing where according to policy people are treated the same but evidently this couldn't be further from the truth.

Rampton can mean different things to different people depending on how you are being treated and what ward you are placed on. When I worked on the Peaks unit, also known as the Dark side – an oppressive area of the hospital for me with very devious patients – getting embroiled in disputes, secluding a patient and helping an adjacent ward to seclude another before lunch was part of a normal day. A lot of the time it can feel like you're constantly putting out fires. In contrast, I have spent the odd day on certain safer and more desirable wards. Once it was explained to me on such a ward relocation for the day, that at morning handover my sole responsibility was to occupy a particularly demanding patient so that the usual staff could get on with the day-to-day running of the ward. Four cups of teas, thirty-three frames of pool and twenty-two games of table tennis later, my fourteen-hour shift had flown by and I was going home.

Anyway, if like me, you commit career suicide and speak out, whether whistleblowing or a grievance, the policy or the truth will not protect you but it gives off a reverberation, an echo and I was now beginning to understand that. A bit like my comments were a single strike of lightning but the thunder rolled around for ages. Once I embarked on an alternative jobsearch, my employers at Rampton made a point in disclosing my suspension and investigation to my future employers – a tactic anticipated to the point that I mentioned it in my job interview so it did not come as a surprise. But Rampton were devious: they left me in a spurious cloud, telling my future employer I was being investigated on a conduct issue and all my future employer wanted to know was whether it was a child protection issue. Rampton would not elaborate, hiding behind the reason that it was confidential. Well if that was the case, why mention it at all if it was confidential? This enabled Rampton to cast an aspersion about me that made people have unfounded doubts.

Again, when I was on suspension, my managers told me in writing that they would be telling my colleagues that I was on leave of absence. These are immediate staff and familiar employees who have been trained about confidentiality. Yet Rampton was more than happy to inform complete strangers from a private firm external from Rampton, give information about me, an employee, deliberately detrimental to my chances of employment and contradicted what they had told staff. That's how bad the behaviour of certain senior staff are here.

This says it all for me, that my employer, a vindictive bunch and across the entire job spectrum, wouldn't let me work, and made sure I couldn't work either. For the last four years they have acted unprofessionally and inappropriately towards many staff. Enforced extra duties, expected me to pick up extra on-call shifts. Made me work illegally and on occasions working up to 24-hour shifts – which by the way still happens. Some clinical staff regularly work 130 extra hours a month, which equates to another nine full shifts. This means there are staff who rarely get a day off in any single month. At the same time Rampton forced a pay cut, and changed shift patterns on a monthly basis when it suited them. My employee loyalty, where I had spent years living to work which helped hide the service's inadequacies, all counted for absolutely nothing.

Rampton conveniently forgot all of that and left an egregious clinging claw, a factory made negative, over an individual's job application. And this is why the more sensible or astute staff leave silently. They know not to speak out in any capacity and if they do they know how they will be treated so they just get that other job and get out. They make no official complaint – they know they will be harassed and bullied if they do. They just vote with their feet. This is where Facebook and social media comes into its own. People appear more open and honest about their experiences at Rampton, and this was a great source of support with my case once it went to press.

My book is also an unqualified layman's view and approach into what I would call a financial vortex where money goes in and nothing of any real value comes out. But where I lack certified opinion I make up for it in qualified experience. If you're looking for intellectual reading this isn't for you. The stories and accounts will rarely provide you with common sense, but it will highlight how uncommon, common sense is.

Rampton is a designer dungeon for a privileged few high profile patients who wallow in notoriety and the many tiers of well-paid senior and professional staff. Because of the unique input, where decisions are made and accountability to those decisions appear to be non-existent because it is considered pioneering, my experiences raised many alarming things, including my own reflections that I assume if the right question is asked independently or for public probity, information can be procured from Rampton via the Freedom of Information Act to support any of my many claims.

You may come to the conclusion if you manage to get to the end of this book that I'm a bit of a moaner. Well I am. But when a drastic change in management and style, which contradicted the organisation's policy, funding cuts hit our services as hard and as deliberate as they did in 2014. A significant change in the pension scheme, a reduction with pay on forced overtime, then followed by a reduction in staff and increased workloads and your employer still expects the same standard or worse, tries to hide the inadequacies and expect the workforce to do the hiding and lie to the Care Quality Commission... An unavoidable change in how patients are cared for that is detrimental to their therapy and development.

Then risks inevitably increase, staff feel less valued, job satisfaction drops, productivity droops, morale begins to wane and goodwill ceases, and in my case resentment starts to set in. By the time that happened – and no disrespect to those who have stuck it out – but the best of us could see what was happening and have all but gone.

They have seen the demise, the increase in problems, weighed up the negatives over the positives and thought it wasn't worth the time and effort to commute to work. Realised they're unable to man the wards effectively. Cuts that only affected certain staff at a certain level – usually the ones who need it most. That the environment wasn't safe anymore and decisions made on their behalf were not in their best interests and were also incompetent and dangerous.

Like one recently retired ward worker said – who admits he was so close to leaving – deciding to endure it just to see his pension plan out was the sole reason he tolerated the last four years. Rampton is a basket case for recruiting staff and this has nothing to do with any national trend. Rampton gets conveniently tagged or associated to other hospital statistics concerning insufficient nurses etc. However, the qualified nurses who works at Rampton are challenged very differently, have little affiliation to the nurses who are rushed off their feet at every Accident and Emergency department or the many thousands of hospital wards across the country. They may be under the National Health Service, but similarities are only there by name not by nature.

A Rampton qualified Nurse is responsible for the safety of staff and patients. They also make on the spot clinical decisions and try to deal with staffing issues throughout the day and the next days ahead. Staff nurses will oversee the general management of the shift on a ward. That could mean a depreciation of staff numbers, administering medication, implementing and documenting patient incidents and seclusions, and if achievable try to allocate breaks out to staff.

The difficulties faced by Rampton are Rampton's alone and to me it is a dilapidation in any meaningful focus on the service and the people who are meant to deliver it. Rampton is now a Crunchie Bar with an intact thin chocolate outer coating making things appear fine and sweet, but with a fragile and feeble honeycomb centre crumbling under all the residual stresses. Rampton now has such a bad name that recruiting staff has been continuous for the last couple of years now.

Application

But before I go into that I'd like to share with the reader my very first encounter with applying for public sector work and the irony and contradiction this experience conjured up whilst seeking full time employment. In early 2002 I had applied for a nurse assistant job at Rampton. At the time I wanted to work nearer to where I lived in East Retford, Rampton, after some awkward questions concerning my colourful teenage years culminating in several criminal convictions in the late 80s. I left school at fifteen and fully expected to follow my older brother into a career of crime, much fortune and as many fags as I wanted to smoke was just around the corner.

Anyway, Rampton recruiters felt that under the Rehabilitation Offenders Act I had served my time and due to this previous life had the necessary skills to work with some of the brightest criminal minds in the country. Great, I thought, I have some use. Now, though, the attitude is as long as you inform Rampton of your offences and irrespective of most offences then they won't turn you away, and there are now staff who have not just convictions but some have serious crimes committed even as recently as three years ago and now roam the wards, who years ago would have never got a job.

The Lunar cycle has nothing to do with Lunacy

After several years of employment at Rampton the nature of the people we care for certainly tests your resolve, the purpose for working there, your moral conscience and character more than it possibly would in other places – without belittling our cousins, the prisons and prison officers, who far outweigh psychiatric hospitals. Prisoners are placed on wings that range from 100 to 200-strong population and supervised by approximately five staff. That sounds staggeringly ineffective. I would say much of its purpose is to deny someone the liberty to be at large, and officers are more of a shepherd than a sheepdog. I would argue prisoners run the wings socially and dynamically and staff try to contain it as best as possible. Challenging offending behaviour does not become priority.

Rampton on a good day may have a ratio of twelve patients and eight staff on one particular ward. This does differ from ward to ward, though, and from day to day, and can diminish during the same day as well. The level of care, the intensity of the patients' demands, you need to supervise in close proximity. This will attract volatile behaviour and risks at Rampton and this is the reason why I think Rampton has a greater danger. With variable degrees on the clinical wards you are an arbitrator between patient squabbles, a counsellor, a facilitator, a negotiator and de-escalator where you defuse potential situations and challenge inappropriate behaviour, an enforcer of ward rules and peace keeper. The North Nottinghamshire area has five prisons within a twenty-mile radius and the staff employed at those places, some of whom made the transfer to Rampton, that I have met tend to agree with me when we compare working practices and notes.

Built in 1912 as the sister asylum for Broadmoor, Rampton Hospital was built deliberately and remotely to accommodate the mentally disturbed and in rural Nottinghamshire it is the local area's biggest employer. Although numbers fluctuate, Rampton employs directly and indirectly well over two thousand people which resides under the Notts Healthcare Trust so there is sizeable influence from outside the perimeter fence from offices that sit peacefully thirty five miles away in a leafy suburb, Mapperley, in the city of Nottingham.

The word asylum has become a dirty word to the point of being an obsolete term and when used, it's automatically controversial. It has fallen out of fashion with politically correct thinking. However, to me the change is politically incorrect. The Asylum definition is a place of shelter and protection or a place someone is committed to due to mental illness. This is where I begin to understand why the name may have fallen out of favour. There are plenty of patients who are not mentally ill or receive prescribed drugs but reside under various Mental Health Acts and Hospital orders. A new category of person arrived some 25 years ago which became a steady influx in the form of the personality disordered patient. In simple terms, to me and a lot of clinical staff I have had the pleasure to share a shift with, these patients are the bad not the mad. The self-absorbed individual. Narcissistic, who only wants to do things their own way for self-gratification. Where the word 'no' does not feature in their vocabulary. These people are naturally angry and defiant to the point they lurch from one paroxysm to the next, and staff are just managing one behaviour after another. Patients test and probe at every rule and boundary, looking for weaknesses in people's personalities and in the system that they uphold. If you are not wrestling with them physically then you are wrestling with them psychologically.

Some can lie in a polygraph and it remain undetected, but a psychopath can tell the truth and the polygraph will think it's a lie.

These people often can evade the intention of a polygraph that uses physiological indicators such as pulse, blood pressure that can be emitted from the emotions of guilt and shame to determine if somebody is telling the truth. But the high functioning, above-average, intelligent beings that cause so many problems in the prison system somebody has massaged and manipulated their file into a person who has mental health issues, needs a doctor that only nurses people from the neck up. Patients often come with conditions related to the autistic spectrum, like Asperger's and compulsive disorders. These diagnoses often become an excuse instead of a reason. Quite a few patients in my view tend to transfer from prison because they constantly plot and scheme, have caused fires, taken hostages, created riots, and constantly need to be segregated. They just take up too much time and resources for the depleted, overworked prison officers and the system they reside in to cope with. Prisons do not punish or rehabilitate the majority of prisoners, they give society respite from a criminal until he is released again. And often they fall straight back into their old ways until picked up again. Rampton shares a similar fate albeit indirectly in that patients who for a time may have been an inmate will eventually go to a medium secure unit and eventually get out.

The mentally ill, however, differ again as they reside in a more mental and physical unpredictable spectrum. Mad patients rarely ever go to the gym and weight train or power lift. Yet they are often stronger with no exception to gender. Behavioural Endurance often outstrips the PD patient as well. I have known mentally ill patients sit in day rooms in perpetual torpor doing nothing for hours on end. Some grinning to themselves, others looking like they are having a breakdown. Then they inexplicably rise and try and karate round house kick the day room light situated nine feet from the floor. No warm up or stretches prior to a major exertion, and they never appear to suffer any injury for it. To me this is tangible mind over matter. No warning or build up of anger that you might see in certain patients. An explosion of power in only a second.

Psychopathy

H ere is an example that shocked me at the time, once I had digested the full extent of a well-orchestrated and planned incident that came at a time when this ward appeared relatively calm and I was just finding my feet on the wards. This incident is not unique, but it has left an indelible mark on my memory because it was the first time it happened to me and for safety reasons I needed to learn quickly from it.

On this ward there were three Personality Disordered patients amongst seven others. Patient A disliked patient B and C, who were both close friends and from a similar background. The two friends were loud and boisterous of a similar age, came from northern inner cities and had extensive drug problems which fuelled their criminal behaviour. They had what is commonly called Drug-induced Psychosis and their criminal convictions surrounded extensive drug use. They were similar erratic and chaotic thinkers, with a propensity to be volatile and violent.

To me they were unnerving and dangerous, they didn't have a specific target audience to prey on, they had the potential to attack anyone with a degree of opportunity. In the animal kingdom they were akin to hyenas. Opportunistic carrion feeders who gang up and pick on the weak and infirm but on their own they would skulk away. As one nurse assistant said, these two were proper wretches of evil and that was true.

The worst thing is they are not in Rampton anymore. I used to think people like them were clever enough to work their way through the system and outside again, but experience has caused me to revise that, and in fact that we are the ones stupid enough to let them out.

However, Patient A was short in stature but he cast a long shadow for someone so short. He was usually considered a bit of a loner. On the outside he was apparently a pimp who exploited vulnerable young women in his city in the Midlands and would probably never have crossed paths with such people if it wasn't for Rampton. He started to act completely out of character and made a concerted effort to befriend Patient B and C, when before he would never associated with them or looked in their direction. Staff handovers picked this up quickly enough and monitored the situation but over time, about three weeks or so, they became considered a trio of friends. Patient A went to great lengths and gave them things from his locker, got interested in what they were interested in, played table tennis and pool with them – pursuits he was no good at, which built their confidence as he was being beaten by them. He would praise them for winning and take losing on the chin.

The relationship on the outside looked awkward but convenient, and staff eventually turned their attention elsewhere and watched what we thought were other more concerning dynamics on the ward. Then on one such day the patients were unlocked from their ward side rooms, and all three patients were the first up. This was unusual as they were usually the last to emerge into the day room for breakfast. Staff who had just come on shift were caught off guard, but the day room was manned, the patients appeared happy, and the offices had large windows and good views of the patients. But before the day could start patient B and C had moved swiftly, held down a staff member in his chair and the other hit him over the head with another chair. This staff member took many blows. Patient A made himself look like a peacekeeper and intervened and tried to calm the situation and as staff appeared to flood the ward from the alarm, the main interest was protecting the injured staff and suppressing and moving Patient B and C, then bringing order back to the ward.

Patient A appeared calm and became a bystander, and he gradually circumvented the gathered group and moved up towards the office door. The ward manager appeared at the window and then rushed out on to the ward. This required for her to unlock, open, then lock the office door. Patient A picked his moment well then with as much ferocity as he could muster, punched the ward manager several times until intercepted by staff.

All three were moved off the ward onto other separate wards to be secluded. And so began the task of analysing and coming to terms with what appeared to be an unprovoked attack on two staff members. As you can imagine there is the shock of what was an unprovoked incident where it was hard to pinpoint any antecedent or escalation, considering staff shifts had just changed and patients had only just emerged from a good night's sleep.

After several days of patients' confinement the patients started to open up and became engaging with staff. Staff took turns to sit outside seclusion which is the norm and were specifically asked to encourage dialogue about the incident. We as a collective team began to build a picture of the three patients all being keen to initially blame each other for what took place. The picture started to materialise though that Patient A had groomed and befriended the other two patients in order to organise a riot as a decoy for him to get close to the real target: the unsuspecting ward manager. A plan that was hatched a month prior, when Patient A was mistreated according to him by the ward manager over another separate, but in my view a trivial, issue.

Patient A's planning showed significant mental stamina, a focus and determination of a high degree – in order to groom two other patients, he completely changed his personality on the ward for six whole weeks to become that person. I thought this patient had already got psychopathic tendencies from observing him when playing Monopoly but I fell completely short of his capabilities. I once saw him on the Monopoly board – which as you know can run into hours. He slowly and calculatedly, financially rinsed other patients dry as he charged rent, fined people for landing on his property and when patients started to go bankrupt he would keenly show charity, give them just enough money to stay in the game but only to prolong their misery. It wasn't the result that drove him, it was the controlling of pain and the torturous endurance he enacted on another person. He revelled in there helplessness and despair of others' misfortune that was caused by his absolute control.

The worst thing you could say to patient A if you were unfortunately under his control, and he was aware he had the upper hand, would be to let him know. I sincerely believe that would the beginning of perpetual torment that would only end in death, possibly accidentally. He loved Monopoly and he was an exceptionally good player but he was a white collar cut-throat He did not have a shred of remorse and saw his actions as justice. He was calculated and methodical. This patient once told me that he had committed the perfect crime and being naive I thought that it probably meant a robbery that made you rich, nobody got hurt and you got away with it.

To him it was much, much more than this. Described as a RAR, which stands for Robbing a robber. And he began with glee to break it down for me. He had befriended a group who were attempting a robbery and he made himself a useful asset, invested time and money to win the group over. Sounds familiar from the above incident.

He got involved in all aspects of the plan and became part of executing a big robbery. Probably noted for his attention to detail and interest. He was planning a robbery, but he was also planning the moment to rob the robbers. He had a vested interest and made sure he understood all facets of the operation. His involvement, he said, should always be somewhere on the peripheral or as a sponsor to the operation, whether partially funding it or providing information and tools. Full time involvement can mean two sets of planning and the job was intricate enough with many things having the potential to go wrong.

Therefore, in the event of any possible problems, often plan B is as good as plan A, and for the sake of the argument a useful role could be the getaway driver. Then, once the operation has been successful, there is usually a rendezvous before carving up the loot/goods etcetera. And obviously not in their plans but well placed in yours, you then execute your robbery of robbing the robber. This leaves the robbers sitting on the wrong side of the law and are unlikely to report it. To this particular patient and in his mind he was, in a perverted way, justifying his actions and in his thinking two wrongs can and do make a right.

Anyway Patient B and C were equally as bad but in a different, more crude way. They reminded me of a time I once worked in a probation hostel and unfortunately the hostel front door was a revolving one for a typical person who came fresh out of prison. Without delay they generally breached their parole conditions, and I am talking about from day one. Straight down to the social security office when they were supposed to meet their probation officer first for a pressing engagement in rehabilitation. Instead their priority was going straight down the social to get some money then reuniting with people of their fraternity down the pub or a park bench. After a period of time the police would pick them back up eventually, go back to court, then when they have enough it's back to prison and then back to the hostel. Sometimes in the space of six months. In effect I had a hostel with the same people in various parts of their cycle. Unfortunately suicide, misadventure or overdose were the three most common things that broke that cycle. Other than that, it was and still is an unrewarding and pointless time for me.

> *There are many sane people without a personality but there's always personality in the insane.*

In the 1990s steps were taken to make Rampton Asylum a hospital and therefore prisoners became patients overnight. That still happens like I have described above, when somebody comes from prison in the form of a transfer. Since that transition the change has created a comparison for the workforce in how it used to be run and how it is run today. There are still staff who recollect and clearly remember its full impact. That famous phrase 'the good old days' gets rammed down new recruits' throats and when backed up with historical experiences it's hard not to disagree. Rampton had previously been caring for specifically challenging and managing dangerous people for over one hundred years, and all of a sudden somebody said that it wasn't working anymore, you need to be a hospital instead.

Dress Code

G one are the staff uniforms – or in my view Rampton gave up its responsibility in appropriately clothing its staff. Since then there has been confusion as to what is acceptable and unacceptable dress for work. You watch the droves of staff entering the hospital and there is a full spectrum of dress. The dress code is a constant debate and in my view the female sex fall foul more often than the males in what is acceptable and appropriate attire. I have witnessed drastic character changes in patients when there's a new staff member in her early 20s and pretty with youth – patients become over-friendly to the point of being protective and then predatory.

Removing the uniform has also proved to be an obstacle for staff when running from their wards entering unfamiliar wards to answer alarm calls because on occasions staff and patients can dress virtually identical. This to me can delay your perception as to who's who and what's what. I have ran to many alarms, locally known as shouts, to arrive on a ward out of breath and faced with a scrimmage of bodies strewn over the ward day room floor and I'm not quite sure who to restrain or separate from who.

With all that in mind I have been out on patients' escorts and felt underdressed for the occasion. It is generally the staff's discretion to wear what they want, whether we are going to Accident and Emergency or Crown Court with a patient. The image of Rampton as a hospital is a dishevelled unprofessional appearance and although this may be considered breaking down barriers with the patient, nevertheless I believe it has broken down respect for staff and any authority. I have walked into court in black trousers, a shirt and tie at the very least to be distinguished from the patient. He is handcuffed to a member of staff who follows in behind, both looking like the Gallagher brothers. I find when out in public our image must look very unprofessional. When I was a driver you used to make excuses when people would remark and say they were blending in with the surroundings or trying not to bring obvious attention to themselves, but the reality is nobody is bothered.

I am not against rational stereotyping, or general perceptions – to me its calculation appears more accurate than someone who chooses not to have an opinion or judge anyone at all. That always leaves you uninformed, indecisive and vulnerable.

Alarm system

As a conservative estimate I would say the Blick alarm, a small device attached to your key belt, will activate anywhere across 30 or more wards and other courtyards' educational centres an average of a dozen times a day, could be more. These are major incidents that mobilise people around the hospital. When I say mobilise, I mean staff will reduce in numbers on many vicinity wards to increase on one specific ward. The alarms do not account for all the near misses or incidents dealt with domestically on the individual wards without the need for external district staff. So all in all I would say with variable degrees of severity there are some 45 to 60 generated incident reports a day.

A 2006 report suggested that in the country's three remaining psychiatric institutes, there's an average of 27 incidents a day where staff have been assaulted/injured.

However, one question of comparison does appear often in today's environment: how is it that years ago, a time when there were only eight hundred staff but twelve hundred patients, yet according to many of the oldest serving staff there were significantly fewer incidents. For one thing, patients do not undertake the tasks that they used to for the sake of occupation. Years ago, patients would go out in parties and do gardening and farming duties. This gave them work experience, a payment and in some cases a trade. It reduced the time spent ruminating on patient squabbles and other altercations.

People today in forensic social science are busy forgetting the past and at the same time making the future more dangerous and uncertain. For a start Rampton does not necessarily discriminate against offending behaviour. Patients may injure staff, as they are dealt with but not usually prosecuted for it. Some wards across the hospital will allocate an individual staff member for the duty of responding alone. Others just wait for the sound of the alarm, and somebody depending on location and current responsibility on the ward, like being next to an exit, will elect themselves, holler that they are responding and take off in the direction of the incident.

Since December 2014 running to shouts has become culturally controversial for two very good but unappreciated reasons. One reason is allegedly in the name of cutting costs for the hospital lead payment. A payment in recognition of the danger came in the form of an enhancement on overtime. This was deviously removed but remained on your basic rate of pay. Usually this is for a 38-hour contract. What that essentially meant was anybody undertaking an overtime shift – and there is always a need for overtime to the point the hospital continuously operates at a deficit of staff – in the time I have worked here, there is never been a day in the year when there is a full complement of staff – so Rampton expects the workforce to go beyond their contracted hours regardless. On top of that there is a pool of staff who often work well beyond a hundred hours overtime a month along with their contracted hours and the maths will tell you that staff are not getting adequate time off. Other aspects that require overtime are staff not being able to get a break because of being understaffed in all clinical areas. The workload is too high due to general risks, the levels of staff observations and other duties, or quite simply the ward does not have sufficient of one type of gender to allow breaks for males on male wards or females on female wards.

The fallout of this financial deduction means staff feel undervalued and if they work an overtime shift it's now worked at a reduced rate of pay to when they used to work overtime. This deduction affected a specific level of staff within the hospital but particularly more so for those who had the most patient contact. Thus, the lower paid and those in closer proximity to danger and known risks bore the brunt, bearing in mind that working overtime in no way reduces the risk at work. The senior staff who have less patient contact but are paid far more money anyway were affected the least, which is why they were promoted and agreed to the deductions and not mainstream clinical staff. That's another bone of contention which still reverberates around the walls and halls at Rampton.

The legacy of the decision to deduct danger money on overtime has led to an alteration in general staff attitudes and the culture of responding to the Blick alarms. I have known some staff to not elect themselves to run to shouts in protest at what is considered a hospital-wide stealth deduction that nobody agreed to. This becomes especially acute when you may have a complement of staff to run a specific ward with staff nurses and nurse assistants, considering that gender and skill mix may reduce who are eligible to go to a shout. On top of that there are staff who are on shift but on overtime and refuse to attend a shout on the basis that I'm not running deliberately towards danger when I am not being paid the danger money anymore. That's a valid point but very detrimental in how an incident is dealt with and tackled in a timely fashion.

Other staff may be passive resistant in that they always attend shouts but take their time in reducing the chance of any physical involvement. All things considered, I am certain the senior staff who instigated the deduction failed to factor in the fallout of such an action. It's the usual story – if somebody can make a saving then there is a cost somewhere else. And the only people it affects are the lower paid colleagues. If there is an increase in incidents because of staff shortages and a delay in a response, then the staff member at the other end may be taking extra an unnecessary beating, more people get injured and are absent from work then take longer to recover from more injuries. It's a sad cycle, that does not directly affect those who made that appalling decision in the first place. However, four years down the line and the hospital has run its course because of it. Depleted in numbers, dysfunctional in approach and demoralised, Rampton as a whole only limps and stumbles from one day to the next. The only records and landmarks it breaks are increased amounts of incident reports, new lows in staffing numbers, consecutive days where patients cannot access therapies etc.

The second point that impacted equally as hard and had a fundamental detrimental impact concerned hierarchal support on staff's attitudes. This concerned a well publicised particular case where a skilled and very experienced member of staff answered a Blick alarm from his ward and ran to the ward in need of assistance. When he arrived he encountered a patient hiding behind the ward door who then mercilessly battered him with a chair leg, whilst the ward team looked on cowering behind a locked office door. They offered no assistance or resistance to what was now an uncontrolled area. The staff member was not informed of the ward situation and basically ran into a trap.

Worse still, this member of staff was later blamed for running to a shout and the management's defence theory was, if he had not ran then he would have arrived at the ward the same time as other staff. This was backed up with a policy probably found infested with bookworm under an inch of dust, which claimed that persons should make their way as quickly as possible and did not mention anything about running. This is not a reason, it's an unsupported ludicrous excuse. For a start, something went catastrophically wrong on the ward, not staff running to it. And the policy did not say no running either. Possibly the ward was suffering from a numerical disadvantage or the insufficient skill mix, or possibly both. Second, you cannot gauge the location of every staff member in the vicinity to arrive at a particular ward at the same time. For a start staff will set off from different parts of their own wards, the pace of staff will differ, third, staff can enter wards from several entrances and exits which will alter the distance to where the incident is on the ward, so all these things make this comment crass. Other circumstances that need consideration are how the hell has a patient been able to dismantle furniture on a supervised ward?

Instead the senior managers are always eager to move their responsibilities onto you, which is what they did to this staff member. What was overlooked, however, is that the two targeted staff in these cases were well respected journeymen. Over their many years of service working with hundreds of different staff, colleagues had proved themselves to be the best in men. These staff had experienced the worst incidents and have the scars to prove it, and the majority of the other staff at Rampton knew that. And this was the beginning of a grave psychological doubt that spread unhindered across the hospital. These two reasons have impacted heavily to the point it's now installed fear and disrespect for how the hospital is run. People's attitudes have changed. Ward staff try to be the grey man in most situations. Neither forthright or challenging because they cannot be sure they will be backed up or supported later. But not necessarily timid either, just doing enough to get themselves through the shift. This action alone has subconsciously put attitudes and efforts in decline. In short, the sheepdog has become the sheep and the shepherds are helping the wolves.

When thinking latterly about other insults to this particular episode, is that there are times in the week where patients can mix with other patients at therapy workshops etc. They can spend time with those patients from other wards. Together they can collude and secretly plan incidents. This is in order to exhaust staffing resources in one area of the hospital, for an incident can effectively take place in another area. This then has to be dealt with, impacting on reduced staff levels and meaning it's less likely for staff to be able to effectively respond in time.

"Madness is just one person's reality in thought"

Run ragged

I remember working on A block on nightshift where it became evident that there was an unwritten rule that the youngest and newest staff were usually delegated by the nurse in charge to respond to any Blick alarms that night. At 35 years of age I was apparently the youngest and newest. Although there are fewer alarms at night, the hospital manages shouts differently. For a start there are fewer staff on nights and patients are often locked in. At the time there were three staff on my ward: a qualified staff nurse and two nurse assistants. When alarms are activated because a patient is self-harming or a cause for concern, assistance may be required and staff are called.

This response goes hospital-wide and not just local or district, and can create a ridiculous set of circumstances. If you were furthest from the alarm it could be as much as descending a three floor stairwell, running the length of the main block which is more than two hundred metres, then outside onto a paved causeway in pouring rain for another one hundred and fifty metres to another unit, then down another corridor with steel gates to the last ward. And if this was done in reverse you could enter a ward ascending three floors to enter a ward that may be physically demanding. Coupled with this emergency journey you are interrupted with gates and doors which break your stride and all need unlocking and locking again before continuing.

I can say after that workout and only speaking for myself there wasn't much fight in me left to be of any use in a scuffle but I ran for the sake of running. I have described the worst case scenario but it did happen and I was grateful, taking my charge nurse's advice and swapping my shoes for a pair of black trainers.

"I'm not a schizophrenic but my mate is"

Staffing woes

Since then the hospital's demise in retaining and recruiting staff has resulted on occasions in some wards being only manned by one member of staff at night. This is alarming and a new low for the consideration of staff, bearing in mind if he or she falls ill, who will raise the alarm? In fact, some shifts are now so dire it has been known for a member of staff to sit on the threshold between inter-connecting wards with the door open to man two wards at the same time. What this means is, if a member of staff is tied up with a patient on one ward or undertaking periodic observation checks on one ward, the other ward is not manned at all. The hospital does have a night manager who makes a visit randomly but that's only one visit in ten hours and he or she are only there for minutes before moving on to an adjacent ward. It's a token gesture that means very little in the grand scheme of things. Some night staff have claimed that a random visit has now been exchanged for a random phone call instead. I presume in the future this will be reduced further to an email which might as well be a telegram.

I can also recall on Bonnard ward where to my disbelief I was sat in attendance on a small meeting that had no patient and the Blick alarm was sounded. Staff looked at their device to see where it was and we exploded out of our seats because it was actually on our ward. Once the commotion had died down we returned and re-entered the room to find the doctor as we had left him. He too had a Blick and looked to our astonishment he had once had to use it and the call was answered. It's nice to know the favour is returned. In my view if you're wearing a Blick you're either responding or you're wanting somebody to respond. There are no exceptions, whoever you are.

Hospital

A hospital is defined in the dictionary as a place to care for the sick and that is the first of many contradictions that exist here at Rampton. Many of the four hundred patients are not considered sick and some do not even take medication for the various mental health conditions. They are managed here for more publicly obscure reasons like being personality disordered. This label comes with multiple conditions and diagnosis but to someone like me who has to manage with this kind of person daily, I can replace the highfalutin clinical phrases and terminology and tell you what staff are really dealing with: they are a cunning, manipulative and extremely evil group of people.

These patients come under the profession of psychologists rather than psychiatrist although some come under both. Every patient does come under a doctor though. Not a doctor in the conventional sense, who has a broad spectrum of knowledge, can stitch up wounds, push dislocated joints back in and know which end to hold a stethoscope. These people are medical authors, administrative consultants. They exert their theories and strategies on paper not in person. There is a named nurse on the ward and if anyone knows a patient on paper and in person it's definitely them.

Rampton doctors only nurse from the neck up – and even then that's questionable. They stroll in usually around 10 am – that's three hours after we have started. Once they have used two spaces to park their car, they congregate to a beautiful part of the hospital in a building that wouldn't look out of place at Greenwich Naval College. This is office space away from the industry and practical applications of suppressing crisis and chaos. Some doctors and consultants are more proactive than others and empathise with frontline staff. Others are ignorant and arrogant of anyone's working existence. They believe that they know best, regardless of the challenges presented to staff.

The cells may have an expensive multi-lever lock on the door. These rooms are en-suite and inset in the walls is a large flat screen television that has a Netflix style access to films, some I would morally question. That reminds me: the quietest time on a ward tends to be when Crimewatch is on. Where most patients are in their room glued to a programme that is advertising the worst of mankind.

"Twelve locks to my ward and Twelve to get back. A dozen of those I could turn easily"

Ward Round

I once sat in a ward round on Anston, where all the professionals come together to talk in depth about each individual patient care plan's developments. This usually concerns the multi-disciplinary team involved with individual patients and takes place weekly. This is where the doctor appears on the ward even if it's just to sit in a meeting room. I was merely there as security, glorified Bouncer in case a patient became disruptive. On this occasion we had one particularly obnoxious doctor who was chairing proceedings. People were generally reluctant to sit in and as I was the new member of staff and naïve, I was sent in. The doctor identified that there were new members of staff in the room and that everyone should introduce themselves. Sounds innocent and appropriate enough that he was considering me – until, that is, he said that he would commence the round robin and he gave his name and years of qualified service. Then continued to describe his degrees, doctorates and other titles that apparently appear on the end of his name. People incredulously followed suit as the degrees and diplomas cascaded around the table and as this continued I became acutely aware that this was a belittling exercise for my benefit and how academically inferior I was to everyone else.

Anyway, the other nurse assistant, who thankfully sat next to me, although I didn't know at the time he my guardian angel, was aware of the doctor's antics. Although nobody else stood up, he made a point in doing so, almost to attention and gave a spiel with a smirk and started to describe his years of military service, his rank and the many tours of Northern Ireland when he was in the Paras back in the 70s. People listened with intrigue from what most would describe an interesting man who had obviously lived a life well before working at Rampton. In fact, I got to know this man well and his self-sufficient approach, along with previous experiences, were the reasons why he was a great team player. Not any formal training at Rampton.

Eventually the doctor realised his intentions had been thwarted, rudely cut him short and then bypassed me altogether and got on with the meeting. This proved beyond doubt that this man, a doctor of many years, was blessed with two arseholes. That day also taught me that not all narcissistic, self-absorbed, pompous people are locked away in Rampton; some actually carry keys. Some patients have moved around the hospital under various different care plans and approaches as we have three main directorates for the patients. There is a directorate for patients who are considered to have learning difficulties, patients with predominantly mental health issues and the personality disorder directorate.

What I have found is that irrespective of diagnosis, most patients have pervasive traits that you can generalise. A streak of badness across the board. Then Rampton have the women services unit which consists of five wards in all and what I would say is a very challenging part of Rampton. They are busy wards that are loud and smell of excrement. There is always something happening there, whether minor or major. I once ran to a shout – it was a twice daily occurrence when I worked next door on an all men's ward – and he was the fourth person through the ward door. A patient was being subdued on the floor and wasn't struggling excessively so the decision was made to allow the patient to stand and walk to seclusion. From what I remember she was about 5 foot

7, about ten stone in weight. Six staff set off with her and two loosely holding her arms in what is known as a passive restraint. I had hold of this female patient's left arm. For some reason the patient changed her mind and started to resist. It happens. I gripped hold of her tightly to bring her arm under control and the other staff member was doing the same. That did not stop this female patient's incredible strength as she threw me off her like you would taking off a coat. My humiliation was piled in a heap on the floor right next to me. As I gathered myself up to try to retrieve the situation, I couldn't even regain some pride as a female staff member leapt in to take over and was making a better job than I was.

Out of Grounds

S ome patients are just plain dangerous and have a history of unadulterated violence and oppositional defiance disorder. They are so dangerous that the Home Office have to give express permission to leave Rampton to go to hospital. On one such journey I was the designated driver and was accompanied by one patient with eight staff. We set off at 5am in the morning to a hospital in Sheffield for a specific medical procedure. Rampton Security department had been on a reconnaissance run the week before, explaining the route, the parking and any dangers and hazards that would need to be managed. It was also decided that the three potential appointments were combined into one appointment. Also, one major problem identified was the general public. So it was decided that an entire wing and department would be closed for the duration of our visit. The next identified difficulty was that all personnel, nurses, doctors etc would need to be Caucasian origin. It was that important it felt like any staff who had good tans were to be excluded. This female patient had a long history of racism and was more than happy to make a scene if she saw somebody remotely a certain kind of ethnicity irrespective of whether they were trying to help her. The irony here, though, was she was of an ethnic background herself. We were in and out without the inconvenience of waiting around, unlike the rest of us when we go for an appointment. Three appointments later we were back in the secure van within an hour. Whether you agree or disagree, patients do not wait for appointments like the rest of us and special dispensations and short notice planning occur in secret all the time.

Another time as a Rampton Response Driver I was made by senior security staff to undertake the most ludicrous and dangerous journey in all the years I had worked at Rampton. A patient was due to be sentenced at Nottingham Crown Court, which is an eighty-mile round trip. It was late February, more snow was predicted well in advance for on the day by the Met Office and the police on the local radio had advised the public not to drive but to stay indoors. The security department had already been positively proactive and imposed a standard procedure of no patient movement within the whole hospital. This meant they had cancelled all routine appointments that had patients mobilised out of grounds. That is, except this one patient. I had to transit six staff and a patient in driving snow at minus 8 or that's what the dashboard was reading. Driving through white undulating lanes in the Nottinghamshire countryside at fifteen miles an hour. It didn't fare any better once I hit the A-roads either. The snowdrifts had funnelled the road into a single lane. It was treacherous, the windscreen wipers were smearing freezing, dirty ice across the windscreen and the washers had frozen solid. Once I had arrived at the Courts, driving through the empty Nottingham city streets, the gatehouse guards were shocked as we were the only people there and had travelled the furthest. The comedy wasn't over yet as I liberally sprayed around the doors for five minutes with antifreeze in the hope of eventually letting the staff and patient out. The emergency hatch situated on top of the van was frozen solid and I was never able to free it at all. This meant that in the event that we had a crash and the van went over on its side – which on this occasion was most likely – it would be impossible to get anybody out. It later transpired that all of this was to avoid the unlikely chance of a judge holding the hospital in contempt for not attending Court. This is a classic example of those at the top showing they really don't understand or care for the plight of others and will go to any length to make themselves comfortable.

Patient

I would like to question the definition of a patient at Rampton, though. I will make it quite clear, coming from a probation background, the people we are forced to call patients at Rampton fit better into the category of service user. What I mean is these are people using a service for their ill-gotten gains. A formal sponsored exploitation that has staff pandering to patients' every need. I can describe about 85% of PD patients as self-absorbed, narcissistic people who do not see beyond themselves. They see staff as part-facilitating those needs. More like a butler or concierge. Violence is a form of currency that has value, the fear and power that comes with this. And because this has been effective in the community or in prison, it's not something that disappears once they arrive at Rampton. This way of life is ingrained. I would also like to make it quite clear patients do not arrive at Rampton to get straightened out over a period of time, receive adequate punishment or get rehabilitation and walk out as upstanding members of the community. This just doesn't happen. Equally, being overly nice or familiar with patients, in no way meanspPatients will return the favour. In fact, I would argue especially in the Personality disordered wards these patients see staff who try and get by without challenging anything as weak and open to exploitation.

However, in extreme cases when all else fails – and I'm not sure what that means – some patients have undergone Electric convulsive therapy.

The procedure, although controversial, is used to treat hallucinations as part of psychotherapy. This is usually in another external hospital where the patient is anaesthetised to relax their muscles, then a small electrical currents is passed through the brain that can allegedly reverse some mental illnesses. I have only ever witnessed three patients who completed the course; one patient became a screaming banshee and the other two ended up in a vegetative state. They might have been crazy but they had character. Sat in a chair dribbling for the rest of their days does not do it for me and although being more manageable, it isn't necessarily an improvement. But somebody might argue there is an improvement because they do not pose as much of a risk and are moved out to a semi-secure unit at a reduced cost.

A lot of patients tend to come from disaffected backgrounds around the country and already served time in prison. They mainly come from family trees that look more like weeping willows than any upstanding oak. The many family visitors confirm this for me. Others, however, may spend 20 years or more in Rampton and never have a visitor. To me that's sad. They have possibly been erased from the family tree. I often found this was a form of denial with families who had the most input to form the development of a person into a complex psychopath – they possibly considered it was not their doing and was too much to deal with.

There are patients who do not see Rampton as a stigma that needs to be hidden. Some patients like to remind you of the reason they are there, it's a status symbol that they brag about. Others try to disassociate their previous offences by changing their names by deed poll and there is no law against this. I do not believe this is out of remorse or trying to start again. I think it is so that when they get out they are less noticeable or identifiable in the community. One particular patient did this with comical effect, though it did make me howl with laughter. He changed his name, which was an ordinary British identity, to a very foreign-sounding one to pay homage to his football team's best player. Almost immediately, though, with hilarious timing, once he changed his name the football player in question left the club and went to a team he did not like.

Rampton is very privileged type of business; it is not a company in the conventional sense where there is an investment for a business and then it produces something to sell for a profit. It does not manufacture bad people into good ones or coach patients into a state of remorse. I remember a very sad day on my ward where a long-serving member of staff shook my hand and wished me all the best for the future. This was accompanied with a wry smile and copious amounts of sarcasm, for he knew as did I that he had seen Rampton's best days. Anyway, his parting comment was as he sternly shook my hand, "I can safely say in thirty five years I have never witnessed or been involved in the rehabilitation of anyone. But my house is paid for, and it has a big conservatory. My kids have gone through university so goodbye." With that he marched with a swagger off the ward.

Brute Force

I heard a well worn legendary story from many sources that suggest the incident that I am describing, second hand, came from a time when things were more robust and structured. But more importantly there was a proportionate consequence for an individual depending on the incident. The outcome of which I believe made the patient a fully compliant, obedient and an engaging individual who some say left Rampton a lot earlier than anyone else because of it. Somehow this practice has got lost in other social sciences which prolong and protract patients' care.

Anyway, a patient arrived on a difficult assessment ward from prison and took no time exerting his authority amongst his peers and establishing himself top of the pecking order. Considered by the prison as a bully, apparently, a formidable 6 ft 5 in ex-rugby player, who claimed to have never lost a fight. This resulted in an inevitable incident that left another patient injured and staff were trying to retrieve the ward's dayroom where he had set up his resistance. By all accounts this goliath of a man was waiting and goading all comers to enter the ward's dayroom and take him on.

This would not happen now but at that time staff obliged in an orderly fashion and one such man filed in to meet him. He did not last long before retreating. Then another staff member went in and had a go too. Again, he did not last long either. This turned into a tag match between five or six staff who took turns to take and land a couple of punches. In my view, fights whether fair or not are usually all over within 30 seconds with a clear victor. This incident is what I would call a practical, controlled de-escalation and apparently lasted between 5 and 6 minutes. The patient eventually started to wane in his aggression and so did staff. However, by their numerical advantage staff were getting breathers but the goliath had no such break and was visibly tiring from his violent exertions, and after a clean blow to the body which by several accounts winded him, he was brought to his knees and the staff were then able to rush him and restrain him and carry him to seclusion. it was a humiliating defeat for a patient's pride which was hung out to dry publicly.

I do not know if this was true; I think so and I hope so. To me there are situations where fighting fire with fire is the only answer and it's good to taste the wrong end of defeat even, to balance one's character. Before people start thinking this lack of sympathy sounds horrific, these people are not ordinary rational folk and a lot of the time they are not crazy either. They are often calculated plotters and schemers who, for whatever reason, relish control and enjoy hurting people. These patients do not fight or attack people with good reasons just to win a fight. They do not uphold the Queensbury rules and fight fairly and shake your hand after. I have seen patients try to kill staff but because of the numerical advantage in the enclosed environment, thankfully we make this outcome very unlikely.

Equally, once upon a time the average staff member was made of more durable stuff than the average person. This job tests your mental resilience as to whether you can cope with the various forms of daily abuse. Being targeted mentally and physically is something that is not quantified enough to be a recognised factor. I can recount many incidents in my time that would have benefited from such an approach that's being described and in my view would have curtailed the constant, almost scheduled aggression. Equally I have seen situations dealt with differently and more leniently that reinforced the behaviour to the point that disruption becomes a daily and habitual occurrence on a ward. I also see this approach is better than people rioting in public and then the police are seen rushing to disperse people under some public order offence, indiscriminately wielding batons at people. You have only got to think about the way striking miners were mistreated at Orgreave in the 80s and how orchestrated it was by the authorities intent on harming others for merely protesting.

"Stress is a hidden psychological restraint"

Stress

Anyway, in my time I have never seen any patient being abused in all the years I have worked at Rampton but I have certainly seen staff targeted by them to good effect. Patients will use the obvious tactics, like violence, being verbally threatening and abusive, and making unfounded allegations, which by the way are taken seriously even though it's obvious they're completely untrue. Patients can inundate the complaints procedure on a particular staff member. The staff member in question is then constantly defending his or her actions and kept under the microscope by unsupportive managers. The job is already extremely stressful enough. You are constantly in a higher state of vigilance where you are always looking over your shoulder to make sure someone is looking over yours. It's a state of mind that puts a strain on your thoughts and actions. Particular patients can play their part and target you. All these stresses eventually infiltrate home life – if there is one. Staff like me have gone off with work-related stress and with the contributory factors all the above appears not only unsupported but overlooked. Things like continuously working under pressure with not enough staff, an increase in incidents and the physical demands of that. Being targeted by patients, not getting adequate breaks so it's a full day of pressure. Then tertiary factors of being moved to other wards during the shift or running and dealing with shouts on top of normal duties which then eliminate the chance for a break.

The way Rampton deals with staff with stress is to place them on a sickness monitoring. This is when you have had an absence and you are interviewed by a line manager to establish the reason for the absence. This is nothing more than an administrative exercise. You are then set a target as an incentive to not go off sick. An example would be not to have another absence for the next four months but if you did the consequence would be another stage where eventually persistent breach of targets would result in you being finished based on your attendance capability. Basically, all absences are treated like they are your fault. So if you caught an illness at work and then had a period of absence, your place of work would follow this up with a reprimand of you being monitored and set a tighter target. The next stage is the target becomes less achievable – for example, no absences in six months over a winter period working with people who are ill and are mindful of being monitored. Patients are often ill with something contagious and this can impact on staff absences. Patients are not monitored or set a target for being absent and refusing therapy and treatment.

It gets worse: if you are absent because of work-related stress brought on by the demands of the job, you cannot be set a target under these circumstances. Rampton managers have now devised a way to circumvent the NHS policy that used to protect the individual and put some of the responsibility on the way you are being managed. Now though, managers will reword work-related stress to Work Associated Stress and by this simple alteration move the onus back on the member of staff because it places you back on sickness monitoring. It's a common practice and absolutely scandalous.

This is when the same episode of sickness sits on two separate NHS statistics but is recorded as different information. When I went to my doctor and talked to him about the difficulties I was experiencing at Rampton he signed me off with work-related stress. This is recorded on the NHS statistics. However, when your employer contradicts your doctor – bearing in mind managers are not doctors although they would argue they are – and records your absence as work associated stress, then information has been collated incorrectly.

Equally, managers do not get monitored when they fall ill; they can disappear between sites within the Trust or just say they are working from home. Or the episode, however large or small, is kept unrecorded. This way their sickness record remains good and they avoid formal monitoring – not that I think for one minute any manager would get one. It's another inappropriate perk of the position.

Annexes

However, in this day and age there are still a very small minority of patients who to me are well placed and well managed at Rampton and I have a lot of time for those people and the system. Within the recesses of the hospital there are wards that have purpose-built annexes, on separate corridors, just for one person. Over the years these patients have been proven so dangerous, they have injured so many staff and are a danger to other patients that they live entirely on their own. When I say on their own I mean they are a part of a ward's numbers but live separately and are staffed separately. These patients are under severe mental torment, usually from a disturbed past. There is usually, under normal circumstances, always a reinforced door or a window between them and the staff – and for good reason. These patients are extremely strong and have a volatility too difficult to predict and contain under usual careplan approaches. I knew of one that could actually run around the walls and I would not have believed this if I had not seen it.

The Annex is best described as a bungalow within a ward and comprises small room compartments for single person living. A living room, dining room, a bedroom and toilet all interconnected to each other with a door and all rooms can be accessed with an external door. There are windows where staff can see where the patient is at all times. The patient does not usually have a free run of these rooms and he/she is generally confined to one of them at a time. For example the patient may be sat watching TV in the living room but locked in from accessing the dining room. This is where staff would enter to vacuum and clean the dining room then leave a meal, exit the room, lock the external door then externally unlock the internal interconnecting door so the patient can enter the dining room and access his meal. Once the patient is in the dining room staff can then lock the patient off from re-entering back to the living room and staff can then clean that area up as well in safety.

On occasions staff do go into the annex when the patient is being destructive, but this is an incident where many staff are involved wearing safety equipment and shields for protection.

Funeral

I remember a much-liked female patient who, I would say, resided in her own trauma the ten years she existed at Rampton. She was abused terribly from a young age and passed around her family for sexual recreational purposes. There weren't many days where this patient could maintain sanity. I would honestly say staff were not necessarily there to care for her in the nursing sense although they did exceptionally well, but the main thing was to keep her alive. She would constantly try to self-harm to the point of ending her torment and we staff who worked with her all had a lot of sympathy and time for her.

For someone not an ounce over eight stone she could keep four men occupied by her strength for hours. She might momentarily settle down to sleep for what we'd call a power nap, then reignite her aggression and this disrupted the general running of a ward daily. It was eventually decided that the way forward for the patient was to put her in isolation. This was kind of a room within a room. On the outside of her cell she had posters on the wall of her favourite pop band and football team and other things that you would consider a teenager would have in their bedroom. Her cell inside had to remain bare. It was a sad day when she died and even sadder that a group of about fifteen of us staff made the long journey to Wales to her funeral. All her family lived in the same town, but nobody could be bothered to attend. Just a tragic case from start to finish where in my view people were never brought to justice.

Medication

Medication, or as it's unofficially known at Rampton as the Chemical cosh, is probably Rampton's greatest weapon in suppressing or disguising challenging behaviour and violence. In my view chemical restraint keeps more people safe more than anything else. Clozapine is considered a wonder drug at Rampton. It is an anti-psychotic drug, a positive stabilizer, where two of the side effects are sedation of patients and weight gain. This benefits staff two-fold as patients who have been introduced to this medication are significantly less violent and burn out quicker when aggressive because of the weight gain. This becomes noticeable when patients arrive on assessment wards and after a period of time are transferred to a treatment ward. You get to work with the same patient for many months and can see the changes over time.

What you can also get from medicated patients is an unrealistic presentation of a particular person who on the surface appears lucid and manageable but underneath can be in turmoil. Equally it is easy to forget the presentation of that patient six months after they initially arrived. They may be more predictable, but the parameters and escalation is always there even though generally they have a more workable boundary.

In my view and from what the field of expertise provided in my time here I had no desire to become a qualified nurse. I found that clinical qualifications do not alter opinions; nursing assistants who progress to a staff nurse do not change their approach or thinking of how to manage or treat patients because of a qualification. They do not return from three years at university with new ideas. They do return with an in-depth knowledge of general nursing, the academic side and knowledge of chemistry, but moreover have a recognised level of attainment. Mental Health is a specific branch of nursing and the qualification and the incentive here is career progression to have an opportunity to be in charge of the clinical environment, possibly to understand and administer medication, and of course the biggest carrot, a higher pay grade.

"If you have ten patients in view then ten patients are viewing you."

Observations

When I initially started on the wards I was apprehensive on hearing all the worst case scenarios and historical incidents and they were regurgitated to the new recruits for them to value and understand a standard of practice. At the time a recent incident had occurred and I was informed that one ward had just subdued a riot and there had been a hostage situation on the ward next door. These incidents were well documented on my first week's induction training. And once introduced to my allocated ward I spent the first few days being best mate with everyone, whether staff or patients alike. You want to fit in and look competent and if you're not you at least pretend to be. But these are no ordinary people to monitor. This is the very best from her Majesty's institutes: the most difficult to predict; a propensity for violence and self-harm; taking hostages; and splitting teams to cause disharmony. Remember one thing when on a ward: your pair of eyes are looking around being vigilant, scoping all the people, but there could be ten pairs of eyes doing the same, looking back at you. You may be watching but in reality it's you who's being watched.

A very wise and dependable nurse assistant of many years once explained to me that when you enter a familiar or unfamiliar ward and you immediately notice patients are telling tales on each other, competing for attention with staff, some may ignore each other or submit a succession of complaints against each other, then that's a happy engaging ward. If, however, you enter a ward and the staff are at one end of the dayroom and the patients are harmonious, laughing and joking and getting on with each other on the other side, then the ward has potential for problems. There's an us and them attitude and in a place like Rampton this will put people, usually staff, in imminent danger.

The ward's architectural designs on the newest units are quite new age in that they are visually open planned and the walls curve in the dayroom. This acoustically amplifies sound for the distant listener. A bit like the whispering tower in St Paul's Cathedral, the sound can travel. The trained ear can decipher discreet conversations or at least with the aid of lip reading. This is a skill I would not say I ever fully perfected. But some of the experienced staff may be leaning against a table flipping through the newspaper when really their ears are peeled to a conversation the other side of the room.

The priority of my first couple of weeks on an unfamiliar ward was to learn the patient client group. To be familiar with known risks and then the individual characters. His or her wants and needs, what makes them tick and to assess daily mental states and overall presentation. A jovial patient can be just as remarkable as a sombre one. They can be cues for catatonic behaviours. Patients with multiple personalities may be shifting from one abnormality to another. These are any recognised behaviours and antecedents that can aid staff in being prepared for any eventuality. These observations are the sort of things that get handed over on shift changes.

This is why it is so important to become familiar with the patient's index offence. This is usually the offence that committed him or her to Rampton in the first place. Sometimes you can read the files and get a flavour of a young person who became worse as time went on, the crimes intensified and became more frequent.

On rare occasions, though, I have worked with patients who are the other way round, who were identified early for what would be considered at Rampton trivial offences but then became repeat serious offenders once in the system. Did we catch them at the right time or is our approach increasing the propensity to commit more crime? Any offence can, in theory, have you qualifying for Rampton and you can have the equivalent people in prison for the same or similar offence but not sectioned. The difference here may be the way in which a crime is committed instead. For instance, a person may have murdered in cold blood and could go to prison and another person commit the same crime but then go further and chop the body up and eat it. And after an assessment arrive at Rampton.

Searches

To adhere to ward rules patients are randomly searched along with their rooms. This can be once or twice a week on top of standard searches when patients arrive and leave a ward. On one ward I considered myself an old sweat concerning searches and one particular patient befriended me in a way that we were comfortable in each other's presence. He had time for me talking about football and I had time for him. He didn't pose many problems to staff and he was generally considered settled, engaging with his therapy, utilising any chance for sports activities. Then one day my pride was seriously shattered when a team leader took me into an office and explained that certain items were being moved on and off the ward, pens and pencils which in the wrong hands could be fatal.

I was basically told that I was being groomed by this patient because, to put it bluntly, my body searches were substandard. And in retrospect they were. The patient would always approach me when I was on shift, have a conversation to befriend and distract me, even tell me to be careful of his right leg because of an injury he claimed to have got from five-a-side the day before, when really a pen had been pushed down his sock, and the staff member from another area entered by the patient had found it in his thorough search. Embarrassing for me. Worse still was another patient had put him up to it and that patient would have fashioned it into a sharp weapon and used it against staff.

Fallon Report

The Fallon enquiry of 1999, which later delivered a report, is an integral part of familiarising your working practice and it highlighted problems that took place at another psychiatric hospital. The basis of the report conducted by QC Peter Fallon found financial irregularities and uncovered an appalling catalogue of mismanagement, and described in detail an incident that took years in the making which eventually led to a major serious incident. The story told to us new recruits was described in Quentin Tarantino style by being explained back to front.

The result of such an incident was where a dangerous sex offender patient had managed to be allowed to be alone with an 8 year old girl at the institute and a separate incident where she also visited another patient who had already kidnapped, molested and raped a 13 year old boy. There were twelve main disturbing revelations ranging from the above to general abandonment of basic duties from searching patients to patients being allowed to roam around unaccounted for within the hospital.

On reflection the investigation unearthed a timeline evolution of cultural norms that steadily became accepted over a long period of time. Staff broke boundaries and became overfamiliar with the patient group.

To go into some detail, initially this steady erosion of practice possibly started with patients sharing cigarettes with staff, staff becoming overfamiliar and trusting patients with keys allowing themselves to be groomed to the point of becoming ineffective in their workplace. The unfortunate thing about reports seem to be that when it affects patients directly, more attention is paid to the situation. Whereas with staff I would imagine it would have to take a death at Rampton before somebody would look into anything.

Staff

To me, staff on the shop floor – that's any personnel in regular daily physical contact with patients – are worth their weight in gold. It does come with a certain set of problems though. Rampton is notorious for extramarital relationships and staff who through the course of time in their careers may have ex-husbands and wives, and several family members working at Rampton. This adds to what is already extremely complex social dynamics when placing a member of staff on a ward. It has to be considered prior to deployment whether that staff member does have a girlfriend or boyfriend, a husband or wife, a sister or brother, a son or daughter, or for that matter an acrimonious ex on the same or adjacent ward. Again, consideration has to be taken for who can run from their ward to another ward and vice versa with such a relationship on duty that day. The thinking here is it is deemed inappropriate in cases when family members might run to those wards and be met with a loved one getting hurt to the extent that it causes another incident.

Relationships which are generally assumed to be intimate occur in every place of work, but the impact is magnified in a high secure, highly charged setting like Rampton. And to me the cause is the environment. When you spend an entire shift sat next to the opposite sex in a dayroom, sharing general duties, monitoring patients, observing staff entering and exiting the ward for many hours often in a low stimulus environment, you have innocent chats about the job and life. In fact, I will admit that just like the attention paid to patients you get to know people completely and in some cases better than your own partners. And if you have made a career of working at Rampton, you may have accumulated a publicly owned personal file of your love and sex life. Having three ex-wives over thirty-five years working at the same place will follow you like the Ebola virus onto every new placement or ward. Just as an opinion, I find male staff more likely to be inappropriate and distracted by the attendance of female staff than their counterparts.

Blue Jay

The most absurd day of my working life at Rampton happened on E Block and in my view it wasn't the patient. It was an indication of how ridiculous our purpose as staff has become at Rampton. There is no conscience of expectation this place can demand on anyone or anything at any time. I was given very short notice that there would be a wedding held in the main Hall by one of the ward patients, and that as a staff member I would be on duty allbeit dressed accordingly for such an occasion. I wasn't asked, I was told.

The patient in question on my ward had some time before been relocated to Rampton from Broadmoor for apparently having an inappropriate relationship with a staff member. Not sure if it was more his fault or hers, but the decision was taken for the relocation. Then it became known through visits that this member of staff came to visit our patient most weeks for several months. It wasn't much fun as an observer sat in the visiting room with a newspaper and a cup of tea whilst the pair did everything accept shag. Anyhow, staff were informed that they were to be married and that Rampton would facilitate as an appropriate venue. Better still, this event fully impacted on many departments. For a start the kitchen staff worked their arses off to provide an amazing buffet spread and wedding cake as well as the usual day-to-day feeding staff and patients.

The ridiculous irony of relocating the patient to apparently prevent a relationship was now officially unifying it in matrimony. If I remember rightly the patient groom had gone to a psychiatric hospital for killing his cellmate in prison. His defence apparently was he thought the cellmate was a savage dog so he strangled him to death. Apparently, after all that extra cost and upheaval and the planning on my ward for that week, the marriage lasted a year and that was that.

This was the same ward where on Christmas Day, which by all intents and purposes feels like a weekend at Rampton, patients were given half a roast duck each as a main course meal. Patients get the opportunity to select from a menu from the day before showing what meals they want the next day and this comes with a selection. So it came as a surprise that when I was dishing up the meals from the hatch dining room four of the patients had changed their mind and did not want their meal after all. If that wasn't bad enough, the patients then demanded to witness the entire meal being binned in their attendance. This was endorsed by the ward manager and I reluctantly scraped four plates of Duck in orange sauce with potatoes and veg and watched it disappear into a bin liner. That one action where the cooks, who I regard highly at Rampton, cooked and presented what I would call an expensive and elaborate meal. Patients who are rarely grateful were indulged to act badly and not only wasted staff's time and effort but two ducks were slaughtered, cooked and binned for nothing other than patients' amusement. Completely insane.

But there are daily dietary requirements for patients that exceed the ward budgets where devious patients have been allowed to become special or different to others. Some patients will claim to be of Muslim faith, therefore only eat Halal meals so as to observe the rules of Islam. In reality, though, these patients are not from this background, not that I am saying they can't. But they have little or no change in existing behaviours and like me often fancy an expensive curry and have found a way to get one. These meals are a lot more expensive and are shipped in rather than cooked on site. It's another financial burden being placed on Rampton and the public purse. If my sources are correct, to feed patients has become another annual overspend, to – excuse the pun – feed another absurdity.

Cuffed to a Coma

Another situation that makes me chuckle for being so ridiculous but in a different way was the time a patient became extremely poorly and was rushed to hospital in an ambulance. This is a logistical nightmare as an ambulance will have a limit on how many staff can get in the back of an ambulance so some of the team may have to follow behind in a secure Rampton vehicle in convoy. This can and does take place under blue lights and emergency convoys always makes for a hazardous journey. This particular patient was violent and so understandably accompanied by six staff. The patient was double cuffed for good measure. In that procedure there was a set of cuffs attaching both of the patient's wrists together and another set of cuffs attaching a member of staff's wrist to one of the wrists of the patient as well. The patient remained in hospital for some time and her condition deteriorated until eventually the patient went into a coma. I arrived on a shift change at the hospital intensive care unit. The patient was motionless with tubes and monitors and had been in that state for days. Dignity was preserved, the patient was still being washed, had her hair combed, was in pyjamas and fresh bedding covered her body every day.

The still atmosphere with a bleeping of a monitor in the background, staff whispering to keep audio to a minimum. But that didn't stop the patient still being cuffed to the bed and cuffed to a staff member. Maybe my sick humour but I couldn't get it out of my head – it wasn't enough that the patient was in an inert dire condition, still cuffed and now picturing the patient being dead and in a coffin being lowered into the ground still cuffed just in case she wakes up still humorously haunts me.

Mental Health

In fifteen years I eventually got lucky and was seconded on a mental health ward for a year. A great place to work as the rare commodity of job satisfaction still existed here. Some of the patients are as mad as a box of frogs though. I've walked off my ward of 13 and a half hours shift with stomach ache from all the laughter. There were patients of all types. One patient paraded up and down the corridors in a white vest tucked into tight shorts and in flip flops with a towel slung over his shoulder. Although it was February and three inches of snow lay outside. He wasn't going to the shower unit, the local baths or down to the beach, he was coming up to the kitchen for a cup of tea and that was how he normally dressed. There was one other patient who was very reclusive, stayed in his room and only came out for medication and meal times, until, that is, on a Friday evening. His usual attire during the week tended to be long scraggy hair, a tatty tee shirt in frayed jeans and scuffed trainers. A bit nerdy looking, only spoke when he was spoken to. If I remember rightly, he had fallen out with his parents and as a result killed them both. I'm sure there is a lot more to it than that though. We had several of those on the ward at the time. In fact, come to think of it, we had one person who claimed to be the King of Denmark and expected staff to call him your highness – we sometimes did to humour him. A Neo-Nazi called Adolf and a Jesus Christ completed a peculiar madness. Still, the comical irony of madness was most of the time they tolerated each other and usually sat at the same dinner table for meals.

Anyway, Friday evening 7 o'clock and according to the long-serving staff, they jokingly introduced me to a new patient who had just walked out of his room at the bottom of the corridor. He proceeded to stroll up the corridor and make light conversation to anyone who happened to be there. He would mingle with staff in the dayroom and his personality generally was outgoing, the total opposite to the rest of the time. His hair was up in a ponytail, washed. An Alfie Moon styled flowered shirt, a pair of chinos and shiny shoes. He would stay out of his room for the evening, laughing and joking with everyone. Then the next day back to being a recluse for the next six days. On a serious note, this patient had to be closely monitored for security reasons as his demeanour and dress did not coincide with his appearance on file.

"Psychopaths often smile with their teeth and bite with their eyes"

Dangerous

B ut it wasn't all pleasant on B block; there was a particular patient who targeted all new male staff to the ward. He would test them with intimidation and his attention became entirely focused on me within two weeks of arriving. The behaviour of this patient was predicted by staff and I had had a couple of moments already where the patient had instigated an altercation. He would escalate trivial situations and it was evident his intention was obvious – he was looking for a fight. His index offence was true to his belligerent character according to his file, running down a high street somewhere in London where he indiscriminately stabbed bystanders as he went. He was committed soon after. Anyway, his first complaint to me was his coffee was too cold. A common complaint by some patients. The standard ratio for patients is a mixture of 70% hot water and 30% cold so it does not scald staff if thrown at them. This is even worse when sugar is in the cup as the scalding liquid will stick to you.

I was accused of staring at him when I wasn't. Anyway I got quite anxious about being alone with him anywhere on the ward although staff appeared to be watching over me, but this is difficult on a ward of routine checks and duties along with complex patients. There are four corridors that lead to a central rotunda. Then about three months into my secondment, I was called to the office which is in the rotunda office.

A room that looked more like a greenhouse at the centre of the ward. The windows allowed you to look down two corridors and into the dayroom. A bit like a watchtower. There assembled were some of the best male and female staff I have worked with. A couple of the men all gave vivid accounts of how they had been targeted by the same patient when they started on the ward, but it had been successfully remedied. I was keen to know why, as my working life was hard on the ward because of the unwanted attention and always looking over my shoulder.

The general diagnosis for a patient who had known nothing else but Rampton for the last twenty five years, it had not altered his attitude or thinking, he enjoyed fighting. This is the same patient who was sat in the dayroom one day peacefully as an unrelated incident unfolded at the other end of the room. This patient grinned at the commotion and got out of his seat and sprinted over, swinging punches at patients for the sake of being involved. To most of us who knew him well he seemed to have a mental age somewhere between 12 and 14 years of age. Excitable at times but immature in his thinking, with no recognised cognitive improvement for maturity in all the years being at Rampton.

It was explained that under controlled circumstances if I was able to bring the patient down safely in a head lock in full view of other staff and force a submission out of him, then that would be sufficient for him to accept you. To this patient the physical pecking order was all that mattered and all he respected. This was an uncommon practice, one I never needed to do again, although I saw it again once more with someone else many months after. So I walked up to him, something I had purposely avoided and he automatically threw a wild hook at me; I managed to deflect the blow which put the patient off balance and to my advantage; I then got him in a headlock. I took no time bringing him to the floor. This is where he almost immediately tapped out a submission on the floor. I let go and as the patient got to his feet he was laughing uncontrollably and shook my hand.

And true to the staff's predictions, I was now one of his staff, a kind of ownership had taken place. He looked out for me with other patients as he did with other staff and never made a complaint against me again. This practice will never feature in any care plan or be endorsed by a doctor behind a desk. As far as I know it didn't get recorded formally either. It was much more than that it was a situation being dealt with by experienced skilled staff who understood completely the patient's mental health status. They rarely get the credit for comprehensively understanding a personality entirely and by doing so keeping people safe on the ward, but that day saved many days.

As the patient stood there still with a grin, which must have satisfied something in his head, the nurse in charge shouted at him for creating an incident and without any manhandling he was escorted to seclusion. The patient I would consider at the time was happy to go and went in without a fuss and the nurse in charge closed the door; in fact it was slightly left ajar. It wasn't really a seclusion, it was more about time out to reflect. Then 30 minutes later he was called for lunch and that was it. Nobody ever spoke of it again.

I think once I had worked with this patient for many months – in hindsight the patient was testing me to make sure that I wouldn't make the ward vulnerable and that he was safe in my care. My colleagues, although they did not say a lot, I think were quietly relieved that a potential for multiple incidents had been eradicated by an instigated incident. Possibly relieved that the potential for a perpetual problem had been satisfactorily resolved. I know I felt more competent and accepted after that; these were feelings I never contemplated before and only came about after. Some might consider this example as institutionalised behaviour by the patient or even staff's approach was not handled well. To me it was making the best of a very mentally debilitated patient and the staff had found a proactive level that tapped into it and got closest to a positive result.

Gate Fever

Of course there needs to be constant vigilance for the many reasons for attacks, and patients have been known to strike other patients and staff in the name of gate fever. This is where a patient has had a sustained period of calm, usually several years, and has completed their therapy so they get an opportunity to move on to a smaller medium-secure unit. These tend to be geographically nearer to the patient's place of birth or home. Considered a positive move, some patients are pushed to go but create an incident in order to stay. You could argue this being a perversion of institutionalisation. To me it's quite logical and rational. Rampton to many of these long-term patients is a safe haven. They get three good meals, drinks are provided during the day every hour on the hour. They are looked after professionally and have staff at their beck and call. They have access to the gym and swimming pool. They have unlimited television and no bills to worry about. Being a patient has other perks like in being in receipt of Income support even though they are financially supported. There's a trip to the hospital shop once a week and various off-the-ward activities like football, basketball and swimming. On the wards they get access to Pool and table tennis. Who in their right mind would want to leave, especially when the last time you were out you were homeless and hungry?

Decant

The same ward experienced a decant where the whole ward of twelve patients and eight staff relocated to the main hall so the maintenance contractors could make safety checks and rewire the ward. It was just the once but for the whole day. Patients were thrown out of their comfort zones, especially the ones who preferred their own company and wanted to hide away behind a door of their room. One patient I would describe as an insane person with bouts of sanity, he methodically measured out a square to the scale of his sideroom. And with his property he brought with him put things in places where they would be as if he was still on the ward in his side room. Although comical, these were people heavily medicated but still consumed by complete madness, looking for some familiarity. Although in a different environment, this patient merely acted out his usual madness and quirky behaviour, rocking and laughing, having impromptu arguments with himself. All things he would usually be observed doing as if he was still in his room on the ward. I remember working on another ward where one patient indulged in masturbation constantly day and night. His care plan identified sexual triggers as the section of womenswear in a communal catalogue. And watching television and female staff. But in all honesty, it was something he did anyway. The only thing that was reduced was discretion. He would often be sent to his side room where he still had to be observed every ten minutes and his masturbation would continue there instead.

Security

If I have a lock that can be opened by many keys, it's a minor lock. But if I have a key that can open many locks it's a Master key.

One liberty that is given up by all professions are security searches. Every person entering Rampton is subject to a search. And an identification check. The system has flaws but the security in Rampton is of an exceptional level compared to prisons and medium-secure units I have entered around the country.

Staff culture of fear

A well-documented incident in the last few years can aptly describe the fear that staff are now working under and considering a timeline concerning decline I would say it has been particularly bad since 2014. I know of a staff member of proven years at Rampton, whom I have had the pleasure to work with in the worst scenarios. He began to feel anxious in managing his duties and the ward he was responsible for. This was because of daily low staffing levels and skill mixes on his ward. To the point it became regular and thus a normal problem.

Firstly – and in my experience the majority of staff have all done this – you arrive at the beginning of your shift and go through the staff search system at reception. This will also identify you as a person and allow you to pick up a set of highly sophisticated security keys. There is an area in this process that will give you an opportunity to see on a large sheet of paper where you have been distributed for the day. Staff cannot take it for granted they they will automatically be on their own ward, although there are staff who never move and some who appear to always be moved.

Equally if you are on overtime then you need to know where you have been allocated for the day because that could be anywhere in the hospital. This chart provides information for all staff on all wards.

Generally, there is attention paid to ensuring a qualified nurse, the right gender mix i.e. an easy example not too many men on a women's ward and not too many women on an all-male ward. However, that does not mean it does not happen.

I have been in a situation where you arrive at work and look at the rota. A complement list of staff and qualification banding. Certain emotions can enter your head. You may feel reassured the numbers are adequate, the mix is good, there are strong characters, a sound physical presence that will reinforce the ward rules and keep staff safe. You can also have the feeling of anxiety that in your view the team is particularly weak to deal with certain situations and that the patients are well aware and will attempt to exploit this. This would alter my decision-making for the day. I would become inconsistent, pander to certain patients' needs, may say yes when normally I would say no just to keep the peace or for my own self-preservation.

In recent times at Rampton the erosion of ensuring the safety of staff numbers concerning quality and quantity is brought into doubt a lot more often now to the point that ward rules become grey areas and begin to dilute their purpose, it compromises the safety of staff and its patients. This happens over a period of time.

"A death glare is the premeditated action of killing someone in thought"

One such incident took place on Derwent ward, a notoriously difficult ward due to the volatility of patients. These people may be going through a particular mental episode that meant they were extracted from their normal ward and placed on Derwent to be supervised more intensively and some patients are regular visitors as such as it may be part of a cycle. Derwent is a last stop shop; there really is nowhere else these patients can go. That includes the entire country. They may arrive from attacking staff or fellow patients and stay on Derwent until such a time as they are considered reasonable and safe enough to return back to their treatment ward, or on occasions an alternative ward.

No bed on any ward belongs to any patient during their stay at Rampton, but once here, a bed is available somewhere. Derwent usually has more staff than other wards. Anyway, the incident in question raised alarming concerns that had already been highlighted by staff member A some time previously. Despite this, the inevitable happened. An altercation ensued between staff member A and a patient that quickly escalated – they often do and on many wards. The incident quickly descended into a physical restraint. This situation is not as common but certain patients are so predictable that it is less common to calm and restore some order without the use of a Blick alarm, a number of prepared staff, a subsequent restraint and then secluding the individual. This is to give time to evaluate the incident and remove a patient away from the environment.

Now antecedents play a significant part in patient behaviour and records are kept appropriately enough for occasions to predict a behaviour or reaction. What I am trying to say is on this occasion staffing levels were sufficiently low and the complement was inexperienced; it actually germinated an incident and nurtured a nasty moment. The problem here is the experienced staff who were in short supply were powerless to tackle this appropriately and when they attempted to it was too late.

This process of challenging patients is volatile and unpredictable, even when planning tactically for such incidents. For a start, to tackle a patient it is considered ideal to have four staff members to physically bring a patient under safe restraint. An example is one person on each limb and other staff escorting you through doors etc. This gives the opportunity for staff to use approved locks in subduing and transiting patients and staff safely. Training is provided annually and updated for this procedure. Techniques can alter from year to year but the training in my time has basically remained the same.

Again in an ideal situation there are sufficient numbers. When I say that, I mean enough staff to keep order on the ward whilst its existing staff are preoccupied with the current incident. It is worth mentioning that it has been known for incidents to take place deliberately at a specific time on a ward for the benefit of another patient who instigates another incident on another ward. Whilst staff are running to one shout and diminishing numbers on many wards in a specific area, then if an incident started on another in the opposite direction, the resources of staff would be severely strained. In my view, staff who are perceptively equipped to such situations, it actually pays staff to be slightly paranoid regarding patients' motives in relation to their current mood and index offence.

Also, during restraints Velcro belts are used to impede joint and limb movement for patients who make the most of the physical contact. This means staff can remain at a distance which makes it safer for everyone. I have known patients to carefully plan an inevitable seclusion by rubbing themselves all over in baby oil or shampoo and strip down to shorts. This impedes grip and makes restraining difficult, the patient is harder to subdue and staff are more prone to get hurt. Irrespective of an individual's strength or level of fitness, this is dangerous.

On this occasion I am describing experienced staff made an attempt to bring a patient under control. Inexperienced staff froze in shock and didn't even press their Blick alarm. As a result, these two experienced staff struggled more than was necessary waiting for the ward to fill with more staff. This delay meant that staff were restraining for far longer than was necessary.

Eventually Staff A, under duress, pressed his Blick once the patient was in a half nelson. Now this move is not an acceptable restraint manoeuvre but nevertheless the only one the staff member A could implement to free a hand to raise the alarm and press his Blick. Bearing in mind there were two other staff six feet away just looking on. It is never advisable to let go. For a start, another staff member who is hanging on also is relying on you to prevent a blow or a bite coming their way.

In my view and general staff consensus, staff and the patient were unnecessarily injured and the outcome was the suspension of staff member A. A full and thorough investigation of the incident apparently ensued, though I doubt it as the results took on a sinister feel that compromised priority and professional integrity. All the blame was placed on Staff A's actions. He went through that familiar chestnut ordeal in being suspended for months, sacked then reinstated with a demotion. That's three big punishments for one incident. The justice came in the form of good representation. That's the eventual revelation of the truth by the way. A commodity in very short supply at Rampton. It's just shocking.

Decisions these days by the hierarchy are based solely on an exact moment in time to deal with that situation. They are reactive not proactive. They do not consider antecedents and long term mitigating circumstances. Decisions now are an ephemera and apply to that moment for that person on that day. Unlike before, they seldom follow reasonable consideration or a proven precedent. And it is these irrational, unjustified actions that now roam as rumours within Rampton that prevent people speaking out. These advertised moments now corral people into psychological withdrawal of any opinion. It has produced a population of stagnated staff who do the least to preserve their employment. This is what the Army call being the grey man. A person who tries not to bring any attention to themselves good or bad in the hope of getting through training camp unnoticed.

The investigation, if there really was one, of this incident never exposed that the ward was well below staff complement in numbers or that a particularly dangerous ward had a poor gender mix and that young staff were also inexperienced in dealing with highly volatile situations. And it is presumed once those staff in question witnessed a serious incident they just froze in fear.

This decision caused ramifications for staff across the hospital because word always gets around, nearly as fast as a Blick alarm. There is always a rumour about someone and something and I would give it 90% accuracy. I would argue fervently that the real problem lay with unresponsive staff who failed to undertake their duties that day. Like staff A, they had been trained to a competent physical level to manage violence and aggression. They too carried a Blick alarm, had a responsibility to others, but instead the book was thrown at the one person who made the best of an extremely dangerous situation.

And this is now the problem at Rampton – you are only as good as your last shift. There is no formal process in how you are managed or any meaningful support for any individual that attempts to do the right thing. There appears to be no enquiry or debrief to ascertain events. Every action and incident is a lottery in how you will be dealt with. You cannot rely on any present or previous precedent. Any erratic decision, formal or informal, can happen at any time depending on what appears in a manager's mind. The security department is given the responsibility of manning the wards to a safe number. This is a pre-determined exercise of staffing each individual area. Then another department, the resource centre, a collection of desks with phones, usually house the site manager. They will make the decision to increase or decrease the deficit of any ward before, during and after a shift. This can mean operating below standard numbers. There are wards operating regularly or daily well below the set recommended number. It gets to the point that a team leader or staff nurse who makes every effort to man his or her ward becomes demoralised because the staff they recruit only get moved elsewhere. Staff allocations follow a fluctuating criteria and consider the individual, the known risks with patients, the ward's current dynamics, the gender of staff, the skill mix of qualified and unqualified staff, the known experiences and whether staff have relations or partners on those wards. Due to staff shortages, the consideration for this has eroded and some of these aspects are afforded more attention than others.

As for incidents, there is no benchmark or continuity in how you will be managed. Staff now have fewer rights than the people who are supposed to protect them and fewer still than patients who bend them whilst they try to keep some form of order.

I worked with a member of staff who did his job to the best of his ability and that usually attracts unwanted attention from patients. If you implement ward rules rigidly then in effect patients do not like a routine or system that keeps them in total check. And if you lack any form of compromise then you are of no use to the patient and they begin to fabricate incidents to complain about you. Unfortunately, these complaints are afforded too much time and money and it was in the interest of the patient that this staff member was moved. Personally I feel that was a dreadful decision – he was doing his job and doing it well. If anyone had to move and be disrupted it should have been the patient. I think the staff member in question should have received far more respect and support in his approach but he didn't.

Restraining

E qually as bad, I once witnessed a patient on C block who attacked a staff nurse with his plastic coffee cup; it had sugar in it so the hot liquid would stick to him and scald him. We all sprang into action and suppressed the patient, waiting for back up. Fortunately, night staff were just coming on shift and we had enough staff to deal with the incident internally. This restraining itself went on for several minutes and it was decided due to the day's behaviour and the previous day's things were escalating to a point the patient was to be injected with PRN. This is a shortened Latin phrase "pro re nata" which means as things are needed. This was for the intention to stabilise the patient who was increasingly becoming dangerous to himself and others. It was also decided for the sake of dignity that the patient would be moved to seclusion out of sight from patients before implementing the PRN.

We carried the patient down the corridor to seclusion. This is usually the last room down a corridor of a ward away from the general workings of a ward. The patient made it as difficult as possible as we staggered and stumbled down the corridor, taking breathers and swapping staff over as we went. Once the patient was in the seclusion suite he then wanted the night staff to administer the injection, shouting he didn't want the day staff nurse to do it but would cooperate if his request was met. This caused an argument among the two staff nurses who had conflicting views in what should take place. The night staff nurse wanted to do it to appease the patient. The day staff nurse, who had been attacked for declining a request, said that it was his decision so he was responsible. This was being publicly overruled in front of the patient. This is a classic move by certain Personality disordered patients in verbally wrestling control away from staff if they have been unsuccessful physically. This is a way in trying to have some say or the last word. The day staff nurse, who by the way is still in charge, was still restraining the patient with me and others. The night staff nurse seized the opportunity to administer the PRN. Once the staff had exited safely and the patient was locked up, we could hear the echo of industrial language, and kicks to the door as we faded down the corridor, as we walked off puffing and panting. An argument ensued between the two staff nurses to the point once we had got into the office it escalated into a stand-off. A shirt was ripped and buttons pinged around the office wall. This was the only time I ever had to prise a staff member off another and restrain, albeit partially. For the record, I fully support the day staff nurse who had spent the last thirteen hours trying to de-escalate one potential incident after another with this patient. At the time a complete stranger to me. The night staff nurse appeared oblivious as to how detrimental his actions had been in front of other staff and patients. The team had split in public and patients had seen it and that wasn't good for the running of a ward. Patients will exploit any avenue for their own benefits, often befriending one staff member and ignoring the other. Patients will tell you things that may or may not have been said when you weren't on shift. Try and get into your head.

Room Searches

Room searches are an integral and proactive form of security at Rampton. They may be random but they are regular. I am a firm believer that they serve a good purpose for the safety of staff and patients. They are also an opportunity for a patient to engage with staff who can spectate his room search if he wishes but must be stood outside his room. It was common practice for staff to show a level of leniency with patients who do not generally pose a problem on the ward. To allow minimal breaches of items within the room. He or she may have more socks, or an extra pair of shoes than the regulated amount, a couple of extra books. Some would argue that these insignificant extras may not help a patient who may think he is getting one over the system and the staff. Obviously discretion and experience dictates how far this would go if at all. But it works the other way too. When patients go into a mental episode or become generally non-compliant, the perks can be removed. The ward rules become strict and the patient learns about compromise in relation to consequence.

Disaster day

I was moved several years ago to Erskine Ward at the start of my shift. I remember this day vividly for several reasons. Firstly, it was the only ward that I had not worked on out of all the other thirty-five or so wards.

Secondly, although under complement of numbers, that's only four of us on a ward with fourteen patients. All the staff that day except one were from other wards around the hospital and quite clearly this was a catastrophe in the making. Thirdly, there were staff familiar to Erskine Ward including the ward manager on shift that day, but they were with a patient out of grounds. And this left the nurse in charge ill equipped for the day. On top of that the said nurse in charge was back from long term sickness for the first time and unceremoniously plunged straight in at the deep end. You knew instantly it was going to be a long day without a break and possibly without anything to eat.

The day was instantly strained as patients' demands became backlogged as they exploited our low numbers and unfamiliarity of the ward schedules. Some patients went to therapies and sport sessions, others remained in their rooms and just appeared on the hour for drinks. It was decided during the day that the entire ward would decant to a recreational facility down the corridor. Quite an easy move on the face of it as it only entailed moving all patients and staff through three locked doors to get there. The standard procedure here is that every door is allocated with a staff member who then counts all patients as they go over the threshold. The door is then locked before another door is unlocked, and so on.

When we returned two hours later we opened our ward front door to a hysterical housekeeper explaining that we had left a patient behind and once we had left he was roaming around on his own. In hindsight this could have been a catastrophe and no amount of apologies sufficed at the time. Once we had searched the patients back on the ward we assembled in the office. The exchange of comments became quickly heated as staff started to blame each other but that wasn't the most humiliating thing. It was a pause in conversation that made us aware of an outside noise. That's when staff realised that every patient had their faces pressed against every window outside the main office listening and laughing at the accusations being thrown around by staff at each other. It was the most ignominious experience ever. I was interviewed about the shift a week later and we never found out what happened to the staff nurse in charge who we never saw again at Rampton. I can only guess that he was scapegoated to cover all the other incompetent mitigating circumstances leading up to this one shift.

"If you find excuses they tend to hide reasons"

Today's culture

I f you really believe in what your ethos is and how you operate as an institute then transparency would be a healthy interaction and more to the point invited. You would not be bothered that you are subjected to scrutiny. Rationality of reason and logical approaches would support the cause. This is why staunch resistance from the senior level tells me they have something to hide and behind the disrespect is an unidentified incompetency.

The hospital is so deficient of staff, and experienced ones at that, to deal with certain situations it becomes an unreliable, reactionary place of work. Coupled with the fear of using your initiative, possibly known as common sense, although I find it mainly uncommon. Staff are reluctant or do not have the confidence to deal with situations and challenge patients appropriately or professionally. And I can give you a very good recent example.

Only in March 2019 there was a shout on Quantock ward where a patient, we shall call him Jake, had been locked up for the night and once in his room had broken his stereo and used the two large magnets on the back of the speakers to smash his way through a window out of his en-suite cell. I know what you're thinking, what the hell was he doing with a stereo. This patient was now at large threatening staff with a heavy blunt weapon. The response was so insufficient a second call was activated, not from the Blick system but via the radio communications which are situated usually on a person on every ward. The call said that any staff across the hospital who were sat observing a seclusion and therefore considered the patient to be asleep, were to respond and assist the incident on Quantock ward. As I have described before, this may be hundreds of metres away, going through many locked doors and from different levels.

On first impressions I suppose the request could be considered the best alternative, but when you begin to break it down it becomes a shambles. For a start some patients in seclusion are all in there for a good reason. They may be self-harming and need watching usually every 5 to 15 minutes. There's a good possibility due to the acoustics that they may have heard this radio call just outside their door and pretended to be asleep in the hope staff would leave them so they can do their worst.

Another factor is this radio call totally disregarded previous incidents where staff were reprimanded and disciplined – even suspended – for momentarily leaving a seclusion observation post, or for just reading a paper, going to the toilet or taking a phone call; and now when it suited, senior people were now openly encouraging staff to do a lot worse, it just beggars belief.

It is my view that Rampton is so contradictory in how it treats people individually that it's immoral and staff have no respect for the decisions made these days. The detriment of this is there was no uniform response to such alarms. Some staff would have stalled in attending the shout for fear of reprisals. Some staff went without hesitation for the benefit of aiding endangered colleagues, and some stayed put assessing the gravity and implications of leaving what is considered a mind numbing and very low stimulus duty. They often go on for hours, on occasions the entire shift, but an important responsibility nonetheless.

Either way, staff are now left trying to navigate the minefield of such crass and desperate decisions. Having to wrestle with their own professional boundaries and conscience in what to do for the best. Being dependent on any formal or informal outcome that may surface later to the jeopardy of their decisions. On top of that, Rampton's hierarchy are now so insular and protective of any ridicule there is nowhere to take any concerns.

Senior staff can appear, on the face of it, intelligent and informed people concerning certain processes like tribunals, grievances and disciplinaries, but what really happens is managers will send reports to solicitors – which by the way charge Rampton a thousand pounds an hour – I would imagine money is being funnelled in their direction daily. This use of a private agency is to research any legal implications. They may send it also to the Human Resources department who analyse policies and procedures of an incident, looking for blame. Then take advice and implement an action. This may appear rational or logical. Then the same person makes a domestic or pastoral choice concerning how to treat individuals in the workplace and the wards, and this may appear unfair or harsh and makes that senior person look unpredictable. What takes place is the erratic behaviour where one decision has been kept in check with professional help and the other is the actual incompetent person. This has now given way to swathes of incompetent people submerged in incompetent processes.

Apology Payouts

If patients complain – and there are many who do, usually about staff, their food being too cold or not up to their standard – the hospital give patients payouts and I have known figures up to £250 per complaint for each individual patient. It's a complete scandal. This is a regular income for a serial complainer and another financial burden on the NHS. It's worth pointing out that when staff are wronged – and that's definitely more often than the service user – there is no financial apology of any kind. Like I wasn't able to get to the canteen or restaurant to eat because the wards were short of staff. Or if staff complained about the food, which by the way I hold in high regard and in my opinion is very good.

"If I can't harm others then I'll have to harm myself"

Least Restrictive practice

The way patients are managed now has dramatically changed in the time I have been at Rampton. The biggest controversial change is the Least restrictive practice. This is where patients almost have a right to self-harm instead of staff enforcing preventative measures. There are certain levels to prevent self-harm where staff actively hold patients down. Self-harm can be many things and I have witnessed the many elaborate ways patients will try to harm themselves physically and psychologically. I've seen patients start fights to get themselves beaten up, bite themselves, constantly head butt doors and walls, stick things into all orifices in their body, and I mean all. Ears, throat, up the vagina, down the penis and up the anus. Have swallowed batteries, razors, drank a whole bottle of aftershave. Some patients I would say have an unlimited capability to harm. Some of the more inventive incidents, we have patients who can pick holes in their stomachs and pull out their own intestines. One patient managed to pull her own eye out of its socket. I know of patients who have self-harmed for so long – and I'm talking decades – that their wounds don't heal and stay open. The scar tissue prevents healing to the point of disfigurement. Some have facial grooves or ropey looking marks streaked across their arms, legs, anywhere. I also know of patients who cannot be operated on anymore because the risks involved would outweigh trying to save someone.

The impact of these increases, another ludicrous decision, means there have been times when the hospital, which is already understaffed, now has to deal with patients being sent out by a doctor or member of the nursing team to the local accident and emergency hospital. That will mean the patient will need to be accompanied by staff, usually between four and six in numbers. They then need to be covered on the wards and there are times they are not. That rarely happens during a shift, it just means some wards have even fewer staff to work with and are expected to still keep a ward operational and safe. I feel for the staff who organise the staff rotas for their wards when a manager rings up and decimates all your good work in providing a complement of staff and simply moves them elsewhere. What happens then, the job becomes demoralising and there is no incentive to attempt to have adequate staff numbers as you're simply supplying another ward or department instead of your own.

There have been occasions when there have been as many as six patients outside the fence at various hospitals that are often out of the county, accompanied by what could be a combined staff ratio of twenty-six. That deficit is the equivalent of running three Rampton wards. Again this never used to happen.

The decisions made to accommodate patients' whims is staggering and expensive. One calculation made by a staff nurse on a women's ward worked out that to mobilise one single patient with six staff, a security van and a driver, to replenish that ward with staff from other areas of the hospital – bearing in mind this puts others at risk that day – to be outside Rampton for ten hours amounted to more than seven thousand pounds extra for that duration in one event.

One particular patient has fully exploited the lunacy of the current times and has been allowed to control his own environment and his clinical condition to great effect. This is coupled with a submissive careplan and relaxed boundaries. This patient now systematically holds Rampton completely and entirely at ransom. There are separate shifts that staff work to incorporate this patient's hospital appointment out of grounds. He is the Apex Personality disorder patient. Although he has signed a disclaimer to say that he takes responsibility if he does not access medical help, but this has not stopped Rampton senior staff rolling over on every whim. This patient has utilised the lunacy that now exists in the hospital and completely works it to his advantage. The approach to this patient in my view actually reinforces his antisocial and violent behaviour and increases the problems that his ward staff face on a daily basis.

He not only chooses whether he honours his dialysis appointment, which usually takes seven hours of pre-planned logistics with six staff, a driver and a secure van. Then to arrive at a dialysis suite with a nurse allocated waiting at a local hospital. He has been known to cancel at any moment at any part of this process on a whim if he feels like it. The reasons can be if he doesn't like the staff on the escort or wants more lenient staff around him. I have known this patient to refuse any more treatment before, during and after the procedure. Every conceivable outcome and scenario has happened with this patient, yet his schedule and demands never change. On top of that I have known this patient to be sent to dialysis directly from hurting someone hours previously and was sat moments before in seclusion. I have also known this patient attack staff more than most patients for recreational pursuit and because quite simply Rampton allows him to. There are no effective consequences for a person who by the nature of how he is managed will not be given the chance to improve or think about his actions. In the meantime there is a long list of injured staff, some who have been seriously injured. I believe this patient single-handedly costs more money than any other and that Rampton are in turn haemorrhaging unnecessary money for the sake of it.

Some people are free yet locked away in their own minds

The one seclusion incident that sticks in my head the most – probably because it was the first time I saw unadulterated psychopathy at first hand and it put me into reflective shock – I was taking my turn manning a seclusion for two hours at a time. The patient in question had only been in there four hours. And the team were taking turns to sit there. The patient was unsettled and shouting abuse, which travelled down the corridors and was unsettling the ward generally. Seclusions in my view should be completely separate to a ward. The patient was well aware that the day staff had left and that the ward was only manned with three staff. One of those was me on seclusion. The patient in the cell, a particularly demanding person who always wanted to be the centre of attention, quietly whispered to me through the door that he would be out of seclusion within the hour. I agreed with him for an easy life and sat back down in my observation chair.

The patient then proceeded to rip his toenail off, which made me wince just watching it, then stuck it into his own eyeball. Then he came to the door screaming for help. I then telephoned from seclusion down to the office to explain what had happened. The night doctor appeared on the ward some thirty minutes later and the patient was despatched with five staff to accident and emergency which was forty-five minutes away. We then spent the rest of the night not only out of seclusion but out of the entire hospital in another county. That is how much impact patients have on their environment.

When I think of the purpose of seclusion, which differs from motive and reason, I have heard heart-warming stories of days gone by where staff have been so badly beaten and have been sent to hospital and had a period of recovery time at home before returning. One person was off for three weeks. The perpetrator patient stayed in seclusion until the injured member off staff was fit and able enough to return to work and let the patient out. This is the proactive consequence – the patient now knows the damage he causes will determine his incarceration. This greatly reduced incidents. This doesn't happen now and I've seen patients be aggressive, be secluded, and walk the ward all in the same day.

Unfortunately, it's another area that's gone soft. But people forget the patients are not any softer, they are just as hardened as they have ever been. Now, though, they have an air of justification because people do not challenge the behaviour; instead they cater for it and that means more bad behaviours, more incidents, more injuries and eventually more seclusions. At any one time there used to be around 20 patients in seclusion but it isn't uncommon to have every single seclusion suite occupied right across the entire hospital. And on occasions whole wards become makeshift seclusion suites as well because everywhere else is already full. In turn this means staff spend more hours tied up outside seclusion and normal duties are completely abandoned.

Also, there are patients who are allowed to manipulate the purpose of seclusion often to turn secret informer, thinking they are better thought of by staff. But more often they just wanted some time off the ward and have a member of staff exclusively to themselves. These periods of observations are particularly draining. If you're not careful you can get submerged into somebody's weird world where reality is a piece of plasticine. Histrionics become your problem as the patient has you ransomed to listen. I always felt like an untied hostage in those situations. You cannot go anywhere as your duty is to stay and observe.

This is why I understand that there was a time when there were fewer incidents. Now, though, I have known patients smear their own faeces in seclusion to the extent the patient is relocated to another seclusion because it is considered unsafe, and then the same patient does the same again in the new seclusion suite. Years ago, this would not be accommodated; patients sat in their own shit and when they settled down and their mental state became more lucid and compliant, they were given a mop and bucket to clean it up. This, like someone once said, is the start of step-by-step reintroduction to a ward and we should not deny patients this exercise to clean their own mess.

I remember such an incident where a patient had caused a fight with staff in the dining area and then ran to his room and barricaded himself in. He spent half an hour abusing and threatening to kill staff if they entered with a CD Player. It was decided after negotiations broke down that staff reinforcements were needed so the alarm was raised and more staff were mustered. When the patient saw the accumulation of staff with helmets and shields along with protective clothing filling up his corridor outside his door window, he then wanted to come out. This is always about control with PD patients. He started an incident yet he still wanted the power to end it on his terms. A well-respected team leader lunged at the patient's cell door and quickly locked it. And then reminded the patient you've had your chance, the incident is only over when we say it is not when you say it is and that means we are coming in, bringing you under control then taking you to seclusion. And that is exactly what we did. It's another example that this approach often gets compromised which creates a whole new set of problems.

Summary

Although I can magnify my attention on Rampton because I have worked there, the Trust it resides in is apparently in dire straits as well concerning staffing, the many lengthy suspensions, and it is not one overriding thing that has slowly eroded a good place to work, although some would argue a psychiatric unit moving to the National Health Service was the beginning of the end. Moving people into an environment that was designed for a different client group. Patients were made directly responsible for their actions as well as now it isn't considered to be their fault. Rampton becoming part of a larger organisation that oversees it may have contributed to an escalation of incompetence, interpersonal skills dilute into corporate exercises.

But somewhere along its way general priorities have changed to the point that Rampton is so preoccupied with the culture of being politically correct and I'm the first to admit the definition is erratic. Things like the way Rampton manages recruitment with the use of what is known as positive discrimination. A dreadful and damaging process that encourages employment of non-work related specifics as priority like a person's gender (more women), ethnic minorities, disabilities, sexual orientation, transgender and certain minority religions and in the process it's forgotten how to employ and retain competent, experienced qualified staff who can do the job no matter who they are and what they are or look like. Recently there have been high profile appointments that have specifically asked for black applicants and this to me is racism towards white and possibly other ethnic applicants. I do not believe there are people who would not appoint people because of being black but I do believe there are people employed by Rampton who would not appoint people because they are white. Rampton is a mad world considering the clientele, the way staff are treated which is exacerbated by the way it is managed and the public are funding this.

In the meantime I would say in the last four years Rampton completely neglected those who were already employed here, who had the necessary proven experience, then disgusted with the unpredictable changes they voted with their feet. Got up and left in protest, feeling undervalued and unappreciated and the rest of us have been left stuck in the middle of a shit sandwich.

Above us mainstream staff are incompetent, self-absorbed senior staff who are detached from the history of a hundred-year-old institute and through their own mania and delusions have brought it to its knees. Because they have put themselves first and trod on anyone who got in their way, they have systematically failed at their level which has over time cascaded down to many managerial levels because quite simply managers are not managing other managers anymore. People are appointed or have become conditioned to follow orders. Managers are being promoted for the wrong reasons and the ones being promoted are wanting to be promoted for the wrong reasons. People are not looking to make positive changes for staff's working lives, they want the extra money and control.

When you reach a certain level at Rampton the conduct policy does not reach the stratosphere of senior staff. If you ever decide to attempt to whistle blow or access the grievance process in challenging your treatment by a senior manager, firstly, the complaint will be ignored then get stalled and treated differently because you are challenging from below. It has some form of bureaucratic gravity that makes the process much harder to ascend. It gets protracted and prolonged at every step and keeps on fading. You have to keep reigniting it by chasing it up. Secondly, in my experience the whistleblowing process is never commissioned automatically or acknowledged, and then by way of process subsequently supported. To request or disclose information openly is considered a treacherous act.

Thirdly, if you persist like I did you could go all the way to a hearing to find out it is biased and flawed. I believe I am possibly the only staff member at the lowest level in Rampton Band two who has tried to utilise what is meant to be an impartial and accessible process apparently open to all. Instead you have alerted senior staff to a resistance and you become an institutionalised target. Multi-departmental meetings are held about you and negative efforts are concentrated on you. It's like trying to out-swim the Bismarck. All guns pointing, continuous buffeting created by wave upon wave, the ship thwarts any attempt to stay afloat.

But let's say you have your day and win your grievance. Managers won't be disciplined under the conduct policy so your satisfaction will be hollow. There are no recommendations accompanied in the final decision. It's merely about whether your allegation is upheld or dismissed. It goes absolutely nowhere. It's the same with staff conduct in relation to the policy. This is exclusively for senior staff to implement, not for everyone to gauge a manager's behaviour because nobody is watching or monitoring that bit. It's a one-way street.

It is exactly the same with Rampton's official headed paper that has the logo and various mottos like an Investor in People and Positive about mental health. If you can disprove this statement it doesn't get removed.

It just makes the same false claim over and over again regardless of whether it is true. It's an administrative tattoo that remains forever.

There is nothing tangible in place to protect people like me who whistle blow either. You follow the senior line management structure seeking satisfaction and in some cases it would be nice for just a response. But it is corrupt to the core. Somebody in human resources with cunning and sponsorship from this department generally concocts a case against you and you're removed. You have a chief executive who is often a doctor with a double responsibility as a registered medical officer and head of a large group of employees. But there appears to be an infallible arrogance that makes no acknowledgement for any allegations made. It appears to be more about finding ways in covering it up. It is exactly like starting the launch of the United States nuclear missile programme. There has to be mutual cooperation and a collusion that inextricably interlinks more than one department. This missile launch procedure is where two people twenty feet apart have to turn a key each simultaneously to activate the missile's deployment.

Rampton claims to celebrate equality and diversity when we should really be celebrating unity. Diversity leaves people alienated and divided. As an easy example the LGBT Gay and proud flag spends the majority of the year fluttering above the Rampton flagpole outside the main reception and that has nothing to do with me. There is apparently now a flag for straight people as well and that has nothing to do with me either, but if they flew the Union Jack flag instead then that unites gay, ethnic minorities and everyone on this island all together. The gay and proud flag does not represent me is my point. And just asking the question at the top on something as simple as this could get your employment given the code red. Anyone with any alternative views or moral courage to challenge is discouraged as much as possible.

Once excuses get found reasons always get lost

Information at Work

Confidentiality and information sharing has played a sinister part too in eroding employee trust. An email I circulated at work proved this. The point here is if I ever have something to say about someone I would not hide behind the pretence of confidentiality and always copy the subject person into the email. This is because it is a publicly funded organisation so I assume comments and opinions should be transparent.

Unfortunately a culture of deceit resides and emails are privately abused. This is where it was revealed in my investigation that many emails sent from one senior staff member to other staff members about me for which I am sure the confidentiality policy was not intended. Because there is no transparency. People have and can move information and when I say that I mean misinformation for a recipient to digest without anybody knowing. This discreet action is kept unknown by the subject matter. It later transpired that my name was used in many emails that I had no knowledge about and a lot of it was inaccurate but to the detriment of my relationship with colleagues and my place of employment. Those accusations and allegations were then acted upon and again I had no opportunity or knowledge at the time to challenge it. It only become known under an information request which revealed the extent of abuse.

Managers and co-conspirator departments get to pick an ulterior motive in the way a process operates to the point where, in my view, managers act unprofessionally for two significant reasons. They either have faith in a process but by doing so will not bring the desired outcome on an individual, which is the reason the process is not followed. This then allows an egregious action to be nurtured because the process is unable to protect an individual.

Every word said, leaves an echo on memory

The confidentiality policy at Rampton is not a policy that protects the truth, instead it hides the many lies. When I circulated my information about how the hospital was run and certain people who had abused me with the use of their position, the big thing for Rampton wasn't the truth being reported, it was the alleged breach of confidentiality I had made. In fact, my written comments were dismissed and all efforts went into convicting me. And this is the circus of insanity. The great hypocrisy of our time claiming one thing but doing another. It consumes you with ridiculous actions that vomit ridiculous outcomes. The managers who used the information governance against me were tampering with employees' files and deleting and suppressing information themselves. This came to light when investigation officers were being bullied by Human Resources to remove information in an investigation that eventually exposed senior managers' failings. Under the Freedom of Information, statements and emails were applied for – which by the way should be adhered to within 28 days. However, three months later mine arrived and to my horror an original statement differed to the one sent by the Trust. So your personal information is, contrary to policy, not stored safely or securely. Investigators have since unearthed what appears to be common practice dealing with staff below by those at the top.

The hypocrisy is institutionally deep rooted with Rampton claiming, as does the NHS, that there is zero tolerance for violence. The truth is that depends on who for. I know of staff who have been attacked and the Crown Prosecution has dropped the case, which usually allows Rampton to do the same. Some staff's injuries over time may become numerous but it's not always reflected in patient files or convictions or on individual staff's personal files. Equally there are many occasions where staff including me have taken a blow whilst restraining a patient. A kick in the guts, being scratched, pinched or bitten. They're all assaults on staff but the only thing recorded may be that the patient was eventually secluded. There is an unprofessional degree of acceptance that by the nature of the job violence will be encountered and therefore by its prevalence, it becomes excusable. The only zero tolerance is if staff possibly are ever out of line and the odd occasion this accusation comes to light staff are hung out to dry and like all other suspensions made to feel guilty until proven innocent.

On an emotive level people usually from above can fabricate being insulted in the name of political correctness or to exploit their position over other staff. So just like my suspension and investigation, people were not interested in the content of the information I gave, which was serious; they were only interested if they could find people who were offended or upset by my comments and whether somebody could manipulate it into a disciplinary so as to eliminate any opposition. To add to this insult, when I went to the papers and spoke out in August 2019, the head of Rampton actually gave answers to the press yet never gave any answers to the exact same questions to one of his employees, i.e. me.

Rampton is what I would call a shit sandwich. Patients who have witnessed the demise of services and staff numbers on the wards, realise the reduction in therapies and supervision have more than enough time and motivation to manipulate the situation. Staff who are being unsupported get emotionally and psychologically crushed into submission. Whether they stay at Rampton or not, staff just can't give the job their very best anymore. This has been nurtured over time from a culture fuelled by fear and compliance. If staff on any level become submissive and follow orders and have been pressured or threatened with the sack or being bullied, or know others who have and they choose to comply because understandably they fear losing their job and in time will follow any instruction. A cognitive inertia sets in where whatever is expected is not questioned for fear of reprisals and becomes presumed acceptable and unquestionable. A forum for thinking and giving alternative opinions is curtailed, keeping people in check as horror stories of staff mistreatment circulate around the wards and offices. Eventually, alternative thinking stops because you are automatically made to feel wrong if it differs. The problem here is a double-edged sword that if you don't speak out then your superiors will argue that nobody challenged it at the time anyway and in some perverted thought process it was condoned.

And the one dictating from above, because they are not being questioned anymore and have eliminated opposition, start to abuse their position, become absurd and unrealistic with demands, misspend budgets, make irrational decisions and basically have delusions of grandeur because people have stopped challenging them. And this is where Rampton now resides and an uncanny resemblance has formed with mainstream staff under siege from both ends, with senior staff above behaving just like the unreasonable, demanding and volatile patients below. Shopfloor staff are caught between two worlds, suppressed by the highfalutin clinicians with all their phraseologies and definitions and diagnosis which only repackage badness and the willing patient desperate to have a label so they don't have to take responsibility for their behaviours and convictions.

Managers often think they are your managers, not only at work but have ownership of your life. They do not think they make mistakes but merely make decisions and in some kind of distorted justification their decisions are for your benefit. In my experience, there is an expectation and exploitation in running the service, coupled with their priorities which, by the way, they think should be your priority. It becomes irrelevant whether their decisions impact on your life, for just trying to get time off, trying to juggle being a parent, responsible for an outside activity, being a member of an outside organisation, having a hobby or interest beyond work. Maybe want to observe religious customs. These are very much considered secondary pursuits. I am certain some of the senior managers come to work to create a problem, thinking that this is part of their job description – oh and to feed the Venus flytrap in their office.

But there has to be an environment for that to be nurtured and that is where the Human Resources department have failed catastrophically to regulate and supervise the procedures and processes that are already in place. They have abandoned being reflective practitioners in making positive recommendations having an impartial input to assist the workforce. Too many situations where policy was not followed and HR did nothing about it, or in my view sponsored or condoned it. Too many times where the purpose of a policy is just to punish someone and not generally kept active or in the name of a live set general standard to serve and protect all employees at all times. The process lies dormant in certain situations and is not activated in every situation and the origin plays a part in this. It has a fundamental disrespect for mainstream staff who are deliberately being not only bullied but placed in harm's way.

Rampton is now gripped by bureaucratic bipolar where it appears to have well-structured processes set in policy but in reality it is a mechanism that can be archived, stalled every step of the way which is why a grievance I set in motion in 2017 frustratingly took more than two whole years to arrive at a conclusion – and a pathetic one at that. You are made to wade through the inertia and administrative fog. This is because information can be suppressed and altered. Senior staff always have a choice whether the process is followed and also have license to pick a time to do it in. But at the other end of the same process my responsibility was completely different. I on the other hand had to follow it rigidly at all times and within the specified times given, or it would be automatically shut down.

Then there are twelve trade unions officially recognised by the National Health Service, in this case just three with any membership clout at Rampton. The Royal College of Nursing, Unison and the POA. The workshop representatives of those unions who worked in the field at Rampton fell under managers' coercive control, were targeted to the point they became small in numbers and ineffective in challenging managers and either became subservient to preserve their jobs or left. The incidents or the need for representation did not decrease and I suspect went the other way. There are now only three workshop representatives at Rampton to cover over two thousand employees to challenge what still are a ruthless, unscrupulous bunch of senior managers.

About four in all at the top of their departments. These people from the top of Human Resources, Clinical managers and senior security have imposed unquestionable full control of the corruption. They have been able to become rogue to the point of feral. Push their agendas, prioritise any personal preferences they have, impose their own interpretation of policies and consequently have let Rampton staff and the service down. These people lack any form of charisma – the definition of which is a compelling attractiveness or charm that can inspire devotion in others. These upper levels are people who run Rampton but don't have to operate under it or concern themselves with the impact their decisions create. The CQC report has remained consistent in its criticisms of how Rampton is now run and problems that have been allowed to remain unattended have a habit of leading to a crisis. The unions in turn over time have become weak and feeble in forming a robust and effective opposition to a rogue institute. For a hospital this size there should be at the very least eight workshop representatives to deal with cases as and when they appear.

Suspensions and bullying are now rife to the point that at the very least one or more staff member is on suspension every single day of the year. Thousands of pounds are being spent constantly to cover this. Because of this dark culture of imposed fear, staff who are suspended are more likely to accept injustices and sanctions in the hope that suspensions and the unwanted attention goes away and they still have a job. And through this management style of exerting pressures and stresses that staff eventually become manufactured mental health cases themselves. There are many staff and colleagues who have episodes of work-related stress and links where staff have become mentally ill and have left. I know of a case where staff have been sectioned under the Mental Health Act and one even took their own life as a possible direct or indirect result of how Rampton managers single out individuals.

What this organisation does effectively in these situations never helps the predicament that the individual employee has been placed under. Coupled with the fact that this institution has more insight into mental illness than anywhere else in the entire NHS, which gives it a corroborative sinister feel.

All this contradicts alleged strategies to address the Amin Abdullah suicide case in which a 41 year old member of staff was unfairly dismissed by the NHS. The problem here is unless this affects senior staff directly the recommendations never become a real consideration or priority. It builds another situation where there are four walls without a door. It isn't taken seriously because senior staff do not have to practically consider it. And they are under no advice or pressure to. Rampton Hospital in a perverted way is an act of grotesque self-harm in how staff are treated.

Another thing was without any impartial and active union or adhering to their own policies. Rampton were able to impose things that never should have happened. Systematically ridicule individuals and weed out any considered insubordinations. Which is why I and many other staff are not at Rampton any more. And my grievance and whistleblowing died well before I was suspended. The managers who were reported were the same managers who were able to have a meeting about me in private, decide to suspend me indefinitely and force me out. There were able to preserve the self-made cocoon, an exclusive set of liberties that is designed specifically to erode ours.

There are many people who are have been sacked unfairly and seek justice in a fairer forum, which is why the waiting list for tribunals is so long. In the meantime, Rampton's chosen solicitors, a parasite company feeding off another, are raking in money that the public are made to pay for irrespective of whether they win or lose the many cases.

This has allowed the irony of Rampton-related dismissals and tribunals including out of court settlements to not reinstate individuals back to work as part of any recourse or reconciliation. In those situations, Rampton are able to prevent ex-staff returning even if ex-employees want to return. And I know some staff who do. And the general perception becomes misleading in that people were sacked with some or partial good reason. So, the original action of dismissing someone may appear justified when it is often proved otherwise by another independent body. This is a very effective way in diluting negative publicity about poor decisions and admitting wrongdoing by Rampton. It is a great way to disguise incompetence where staff are unable to return to their posts but the senior staff responsible always remain at theirs. That is why Rampton has become a dark place to work. You are prevented from shedding any light about any aspect of the place.

I have worked at Rampton when it was a secure and stable place to work with respectable leadership and people knew the expectations and responsibilities and patients understood theirs. Then in my latter years I worked when people promoted a false ideology with individual political directions which has made Rampton absurd, unpredictable and dangerous; and as far as I can see the only changes are the people who run it.

Rampton needs an enquiry to identify the social reforms required to combat how it treats mainstream staff and I am mainly talking about the exploitation and abuse of staff. It needs to deconstruct from the top the culture and individual ethos that thrive without challenge. If I was reporting about patients being abused, then somebody would be eager to make a documentary or bring it to light, but when it is about general staff treatment then less attention is paid to their plight. Rampton's culture needs to be consistent and fair to all staff, not selective depending on somebody's status. It also needs to re-evaluate the purpose of patient reincarceration right the way through to reintroduction back to society.

Mainstream staff need to do what is right and not what is considered easy by ignoring what's happening around them. Everything needs reporting at the very least electronically, by phone or in ink. All these issues combined have made Rampton Hospital mentally ill by the very nature of its behaviour. Its mobility is severely restricted, staggering and lunging from day to day, carrying an oversized, disfigured tumour.

And that is that.